ENGAGING ONLINE LANGUAGE LEARNERS

A PRACTICAL GUIDE

Faridah Pawan
Sharon Daley
Xiaojing Kou
Curtis J. Bonk

This book has a companion website. Go to www.tesol.org/engageonline for additional resources.

www.tesol.org/bookstore

TESOL International Association
1925 Ballenger Avenue
Alexandria, VA 22314 USA
www.tesol.org

Group Director, Content and Learning: Myrna Jacobs
Copy Editor: Wendy Rubin
Production Editor: Tomiko Breland
Manuscript Reviewers: Hetal Ascher, Abdulsamad Humaidan, Patricia Reynolds
Cover Design: Citrine Sky Design
Design and Layout: Capitol Communications, LLC

Copyright © 2022 by TESOL International Association

All rights reserved. Copying or further publication of the contents of this work is not permitted without permission of TESOL International Association, except for limited "fair use" for educational, scholarly, and similar purposes as authorized by U.S. Copyright Law, in which case appropriate notice of the source of the work should be given. Permission to reproduce material from this book must be obtained from www.copyright.com, or contact Copyright Clearance Center, Inc., 222 Rosewood Drive, Danvers, MA 01923, 978-750-8400

Every effort has been made to copyright holders for permission to reprint borrowed material. We regret any oversights that may have occurred and will rectify them in future printings of this work.

The publications of the TESOL Press present a variety of viewpoints. The views expressed or implied in this publication, unless otherwise noted, should not be interpreted as official positions of the organization.

Recommended citation:
Pawan, F., Daley, S., Kou, X, & Bonk, C. J. (2022). *Engaging online language learners: A practical guide.* TESOL Press.

ISBN 978-1-942799-93-1
ISBN (ebook) 978-1-945351-03-7
Library of Congress Control Number 2021949138

TABLE OF CONTENTS

Preface: v

Part I: The Whys of Engaging Students in Online Teaching

Chapter 1: 3 — Online Language Learning: Changes and Trends

Chapter 2: 13 — Actionable Principles for Engaging and Motivating Students in the Online Environment

Chapter 3: 21 — Online Language Teaching Competencies: A Combination of Pedagogical Knowledge and Skills

Part II: The Ways to Engage Online Language Learners

Chapter 4: 29 — Teaching Presence and Engaging Students Through Teacher Self-Presentation, Course Design, and Facilitation

Chapter 5: 41 — Cognitive Presence and Engaging Students Through Challenge and Higher-Order Thinking

Chapter 6: 51 — Social Presence and Engaging Students Through Community

Chapter 7: 61 — Learning Presence and Engaging Students Through Self-Directed Learning

Part III: The Next Steps to Sustain Online Teaching Expertise

Chapter 8: 75 Exemplary and Inspirational Online Teaching Practices

Chapter 9: 79 Ways Administrators Can Use Online Pathways to Reconceptualize and Support Teachers' Professional Development

Chapter 10: 87 Culturally and Linguistically Inclusive Online Instruction

About the Authors: 97

PREFACE

By Faridah Pawan

"All educators want their classrooms to be lively and welcoming sanctuaries," says Erin Medeiros (2020), a high school teacher at Kanuikapono Public Charter School on the island of Kaua'i and a 2018–2019 Merwin Creative Teaching Fellow. She shares this thought in the introduction to an anthology of her fellow teachers' online efforts "to awaken, celebrate, and sustain creativity, imagination, and compassion in [teachers] and their students."

We choose to begin this book with Medeiros's inspiring words rather than focus on numerous reports about the ways the emergency remote teaching (ERT) mandate in March 2020 left a majority of public school teachers in a free fall and without much preparation to teach online (Hodges et al., 2020). We want to cheer our colleagues' heroic and resilient efforts by focusing on the possibilities and the potential that these changing times have given us. As teachers, we know that reaching students in all the ways Medeiros mentions will motivate them to engage with us and learn alongside us. Motivation is thus the central essence of this book and central to our work in education. As former U.S. Secretary of Education Terrell Bell asserted, "There are three things to emphasize in teaching: The first is motivation, the second is motivation, and the third is (you guessed it) motivation" (College of Education, n.d.). Accordingly, teachers' roles in the process are critical, as their intervention and participation can influence what students decide to do, how long they are willing to do it, and how hard they will pursue it (Dörnyei & Muir, 2019).

Purposes and Uses

There are three parts to this book. The core of the book shares online teaching strategies and activities to engage and motivate our students (see chapters 4 through 7). We begin, however, by detailing the reasons and the context in which these strategies are needed. These reasons include the specific ways the online medium has changed how our students learn languages; the expertise and resources we already have available as language teachers to address these changes; and the knowledge and skills that are expected in current teaching competencies (see chapters 1 through 3). The final chapters (chapters 8 through 10) focus on the next steps that teachers can take to continue to enhance and sustain our teaching expertise, as well as suggestions for pathways that administrators should consider as they support teachers along the way. Chapter 10 closes the book with a discussion of culturally and linguistically inclusive online teaching practices and resources. We teach learners of diverse backgrounds, so we have a responsibility to teach equitably and responsively. This responsibility follows us as we teach across all media, including in the online environment.

In chapter 1, we detail four sets of trends in second and foreign language learning brought about by the online medium, followed accordingly by 21 specific changes we see emerging from these trends. In chapter 2, we provide reassurance that although we must embrace these needed changes, teachers' existing pedagogical knowledge and skills remain relevant, and we can continue to use our knowledge and skills when we teach online. In chapter 3, we draw our fellow teachers' attention to TESOL's Technology Standards Framework and their alignment to the Quality Matters (QM) Online Instructor Skills Set. The alignment suggests concrete steps that could be taken toward continued teacher learning and professional development.

The core of the book begins with chapter 4, in which the focus is on online teaching presence and ways that teachers can present and organize the online environment to create an inviting, accessible, and purposeful online space. Chapter 5 focuses on online cognitive presence and ways to engage students through challenge and inquiry. Online social presence is the focus of chapter 6 and involves suggestions for building a classroom community through authentic, supportive, and fun-filled connections with peers. Chapter 7 focuses on online learning presence and activities that celebrate and take advantage of students' autonomy and self-directed learning—namely, skills that are even more necessary in the online environment.

In chapter 8, we provide several examples of and insights into exemplary and inspirational online practices that can serve as encouragement for teachers. In chapter 9, we share suggestions to help administrators support teachers as they transition to online teaching. We offer this guidance in the form of a reconceptualized professional development framework and include principles for the development of future online professional development programs. In chapter 10, we demonstrate how the online medium makes it possible for us to include many and diverse voices, needs, and abilities in our teaching. Inclusive online teaching requires the support and wisdom of many, so we encourage our fellow teachers to join online communities to gain access to a range of perspectives.

Links for all online resources mentioned in this book can be found on the companion site (www.tesol.org/engageonline).

Caveats

Garrison et al. (2000) developed teaching, cognitive, and social presences as concepts to describe and explain the types of interactions in online discussion forums. In 2010, Shea and Bidjerano introduced learning presence to capture learners' attitudes, abilities, and behaviors. An understanding of the presences is useful for guiding online teaching in general across the disciplines. Nevertheless, because of their origins, and like all conceptual frameworks, these presences cannot capture all of the eventualities in daily teaching practice.

There is also overlap in the components of the online instructional presences. In this book, we address the presences separately for the sake of clarity and explanation, but it is obvious through the suggested activities that overlap is inevitable.

In a world in which technology evolves rapidly, the tools and applications we include in this book will certainly evolve or be replaced by other tools. (Links to the websites and applications mentioned can be found at www.tesol.org/engageonline.) In such cases, we are certain readers will be able to identify and choose from the most up-to-date online language learning tools available by using the guidelines and suggestions in this book. We also limit the application and tool suggestions to those that are mostly free, readily accessible, and often familiar to the general public.

Finally, the suggestions and activities in this book are grounded in and contextualized by specific frameworks. More importantly, the frameworks can offer guidelines for teachers to consider as they decide whether or not to make changes. The pedagogical guidance and frameworks thus provide a "steadying hand" amid a dizzying number of calls for teachers on the front lines to make technological changes at warp speed. The most important constant, despite all of these challenges, is teachers' secret superpower: their teaching knowledge and skills.

References

College of Education. (n.d.). *Terrell Howard Bell*. University of Utah. https://education.utah.edu/alumni/profiles/terrell-bell.php

Dörnyei, Z., & Muir, C. (2019). Creating a motivating classroom environment. In X. A. Gao (Ed.), *Springer international handbooks of education: Second handbook of English language teaching* (pp. 719–736). Springer. https://doi.org/10.1007/978-3-030-02899-2_36

Garrison, D. R., Anderson, T., & Archer, W. (2000). Critical inquiry in a text-based environment: Computer conferencing in higher education. *The Internet and Higher Education, 2*, 87–105. https://doi.org/10.1016/S1096-7516(00)00016-6

Hodges, C., Moore, S., Lockee, B., Trust, T., & Bond, A. (2020, March 27). The difference between emergency remote teaching and online learning. *EDUCAUSE Review*. https://er.educause.edu/articles/2020/3/the-difference-between-emergency-remote-teaching-and-online-learning

Medeiros, E. (2020, August 31). *Keeping imagination and creativity alive (online): Introducing the teaching fellows' anthology.* The Merwin Conservancy. https://merwinconservancy.org/2020/08/introducing-the-teaching-fellows-anthology

Shea, P., & Bidjerano, T. (2010). Learning presence: Towards a theory of self-efficacy, self-regulation, and the development of a communities of inquiry in online and blended learning environments. *Computers & Education, 55*(4), 1721–1731. https://doi.org/10.1016/j.compedu.2010.07.017

Part I

The Whys of Engaging Students in Online Teaching

CHAPTER 1

Online Language Learning: Changes and Trends

By Faridah Pawan

In Washington Irving's 1819 short story, Rip Van Winkle fell asleep for 20 years (Great Northern Catskills, n.d.). Upon waking up, he could still recognize the life he had, albeit with many changes. It goes without saying that if this happened today, taking such a nap even for a month would mean that he would have missed a lifetime of changes! The 2020 emergency remote teaching mandate added further confusion and worries to teachers' existing challenges (Hodges et al., 2020). At the extreme end, teachers and learners had between two days and two weeks to get ready to teach and learn everything online. However, online teaching takes about a year of planning and careful design.

Thus, as a stepping stone to aid in planning for online teaching in the future, this chapter provides several ways that English language teaching and learning have been transformed by the use of online learning in just a few years; it provides a specific viewpoint that takes off from Bonk's (2016) general reflections on the state of e-learning and 30 ways online teaching has changed learning. First, the chapter covers factors and differences affecting language learning motivation, then it continues by explaining ways the online medium can help teachers enhance learning and address some of the recent changes. Visit the companion website for this book (www.tesol.org/engageonline) to access all online resources mentioned in this chapter.

Language Learning Motivation Factors and Differences

The authors of this book take the Vygotskyian-inspired perspective that the language learning process and the motivation for learning are socially mediated. Dörnyei (1994) identified these factors as specific to the domain of second and foreign language learning, mainly the factors that relate to the learner, language context, and learning situation levels (see table 1.1).

Table 1.1. *Foreign Language Learning Motivation Components*

Learner	▪ Need for achievement ▪ Self-confidence (anxiety, second language competence, causal attributions, self-efficacy)
Language	▪ Integrative motivational subsystem (sense of belonging) ▪ Instrumental motivational subsystem (sense of purpose)
Learning situation	▪ Course specific (interest, relevance, expectancy, satisfaction) ▪ Teacher specific (affiliative motive, authority type, direct modeling, task presentation, and feedback styles) ▪ Group specific (goal-orientedness, norm and reward system, group cohesion, classroom goal structure)

Source: Adapted from Dörnyei (1994), p. 280.

These motivational factors and components are foundational in all efforts to motivate students to learn second and foreign languages. However, well-known challenges to these efforts exist, including the following:

- Learners' individual challenges (e.g., high levels of anxiety, previous negative learning experiences, negative beliefs and attitudes about language learning)
- Learning and teaching style incompatibilities (e.g., active and open-ended communicative learning versus lecture-based pedagogical styles)
- Limited opportunities for interaction (e.g., unwelcoming cultural environment; lack of target language speakers; lack of formal, informal, and immersive opportunities to use the target language)
- Infrastructure challenges (e.g., achievement requirements focused solely on demonstration of language knowledge acquisition in intensive examinations rather than language use focus)
- Lack of resources (e.g., limited access to authentic materials, supplementary resources, learning time, interested and/or proficient experts)

The online medium helps teachers mitigate these motivational challenges to language learning. Ways to address these challenges can be seen in four sets of trends, based on work by Bonk (2016) and Kannan and Munday (2018). Figure 1.1 shows these trends, and the rest of this chapter addresses the changes in learning that we see emerging as a result.

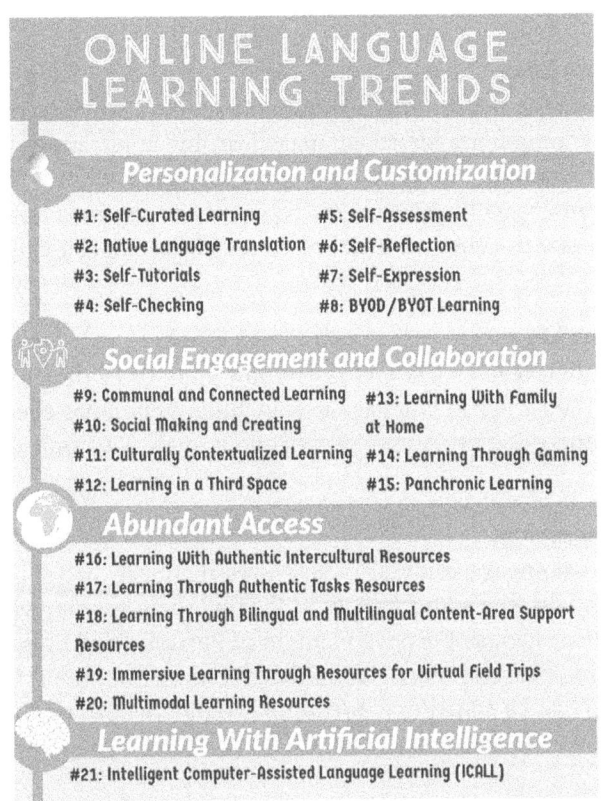

Figure 1.1. Online language learning trends

First Trend: Personalization and Customization

The need to align language learning with students' characteristics, individual experiences, and learning styles is inherent in the first two sets of challenges (see table 1.1). The online environment offers promising ways to overcome these challenges in English language learning.

Change #1: Self-Curated Learning

The availability of online resources provides opportunities for students to curate the English language information they encounter. This online facility enables students to connect home and personal interests with school if they choose to do so. For example, Wakelet is a tool in which students can organize information as well as have access to and draw information and engagement from social media to tell a story through their collection of materials.

Change #2: Native Language Translation

In a time when students' first language is considered an essential stepping stone to their learning and acquisition of a second language, multiple online applications can support this process. Google Translate is one example of a readily available language translation tool.

Change #3: Self-Tutorials
Students need time and the opportunity for repeated practice when learning a language. For example, tutorial computer-assisted language learning applications (Blake, 2011) such as Transparent Language, Pearson's MyEnglishLab, and the FluentU website provide individual learners with resources for repeated and multiple opportunities to focus on, access, and practice the structural elements in the English language on their own schedule.

Change #4: Self-Checking
Rather than wait for their teachers, students can now go to or be directed to applications that support their English language use, including grammar check applications in their word processing program or applications such as Grammarly and Classroom Cereal.

Change #5: Self-Assessment
Online applications that engage students in self-assessment can also support their English language use, with the added benefit of making their learning visible over time. Established e-portfolios, such as European Language Portfolio and LinguaFolio, can show students' learning progress. Free standardized tests such as the Education First Standard English Test can be added to e-portfolios so students can track their own progress.

Change #6: Self-Reflection
The ability to learn anywhere at any time, combined with the asynchronous affordance of online learning, creates room for extended deliberation (Pawan, 2017). The online medium reversed the ephemerality of ideas and perhaps can contribute to not only substance but also precision in communication.

Change #7: Self-Expression
The multimodality of the online medium enables learners to express themselves multimodally as well. For example, when students are learning to communicate through writing, the online medium provides ways of communicating that are unique, nuanced, and reflective of who students are. Favilla (2017, para. 5) points to Twitter users' use of "emojis, new-fangled punctuations such as quirky tilde pair, full.stops.in.between. words for emphasis" as examples of self-expression that do not abide by prescriptive grammar rules but are effective in helping writers connect meaningfully with their intended readers.

Change #8: Bring-Your-Own-Device (BYOD)/Bring-Your-Own Technology (BYOT) Learning
Students learning online use their own devices or technologies, including smartphones, iPads, laptops, iPods, and more. As a result of this change, student-directed language learning takes the form of students choosing to use familiar devices and deciding how to access, collect, organize, and share their learning.

Second Trend: Social Engagement and Collaboration

From a sociocultural perspective, language learning is mediated by engagement with others, which pushes students one step beyond their abilities. The online medium facilitates student collaboration in real and "imagined" communities near and far.

Change #9: Communal and Connected Learning
Social media tools such as Twitter, Instagram, Facebook, and Discord enable students to engage with communities of learners within and beyond their immediate confines. Community building is also a central feature of learning management systems such as Canvas, Blackboard, and Moodle.

Change #10: Social Making and Creating
The connected nature of the online medium gives learners the chance to experience the essence of the "makers" movement—namely, the joy of making and sharing artifacts with others. For example, Loom allows students to create and annotate videos easily, whereas Book Creator enables students to create and share books in multiple languages.

Change #11: Culturally Contextualized Learning
The online medium creates pathways for students' Funds of Knowledge (Moll et al., 1992) to make their way into students' English language learning through familiar information from their backgrounds. For example, the Fable Cottage website has English versions of tales originally written in French, German, Italian, and Spanish. Students can watch and listen to stories in their first language, then watch them with English subtitles and voiceovers.

Change #12: Learning in a Third Space
In Kramsch's (1993) view, the online environment is where language learners explore their insider's view of the first language and their outsider's view of the target language. The online medium can serve as a space for this exploration, as learners can "lurk" in safety and engage anonymously if they choose to do so. The online medium thus serves as a third or available space that enables language learners to explore new identities and cultural awareness during their English language learning.

Change #13: Learning With Family at Home
The online medium facilitates the home-school connection through applications that allow family members to join students in language learning. For example, the award-winning Read Conmigo program features creative and engaging stories that learners and their parents can read aloud together in both Spanish and English. Amrita Learning is a mobile application designed to help newly literate adults at home so they can, in turn, support their language learners.

Change #14: Learning Through Gaming
James Gee (2003) sees digital learning games as having the potential for students to learn through entertainment and pleasure, as well as interaction and collaboration with other gamers. For example, the *Lost Words of Atlantis* is an adventure game based on decoding a mysterious language. Other learning games can be found in ESL Games World, Educandy, and ESL Games Plus.

Change #15: Panchronic Learning
Learning to write panchronically involves the full acceptance and anticipation of the participation of others (Crystal, 2011). The main difference between the panchronic process and other writing processes is that the panchronic process can be indefinite and open, as in the case of writing entries for Wikipedia or Write the World, a global online writing community for teens.

Third Trend: Abundant Access
The "pedagogy of abundance" (Weller, 2011) is an approach to teaching in a context where content is pervasive. In this view, the teacher should prioritize students having access to resources so they can take charge of their heutagogical learning (Kenyon & Hase, 2001), as there is no expectation that teachers or experts—or anyone, for that matter—know everything or have all the answers.

Change #16: Learning With Authentic Intercultural Resources
One of the biggest challenges of learning second or foreign languages, including English, is access to realia. Multiple websites provide means to overcome this challenge, including International Children's Digital Library (hosted by the University of Maryland), which has books from across the world's cultures and regions; National Geographic Learning—English Learning, which has resources from English-speaking regions and beyond; and PBS LearningMedia's curated resource list. There are also resources for various dialects of English, such as We Speak NYC and English, Baby! for slang and idiosyncratic expressions.

Change #17: Learning Through Authentic Tasks Resources
One challenge for language learning is that the language is meaningless if it is only used hypothetically. The online medium provides resources that can engage students in learning through real-world tasks. For example, the Google for Education website has project-based, video-based resources for applied digital skills such as résumé writing and interview skills for adults, and the interactive, award-winning Banzai online course provides a collection of real-world examples for learners in different grades to learn English while acquiring financial literacy.

Change #18: Learning Through Bilingual and Multilingual Content-Area Support Resources
In content-based instruction, the English language is taught in tandem with content so that language and academic achievement can be jointly sustained. Resources are available in most subject areas for students to learn language through content areas. For example, bilingual guidance is available at Math TV, which has about 2,000 videos; Math2.org, which provides bilingual mathematical charts; Learning Upgrade, which offers bilingual GED preparation for adults; and iCivics, which offers materials and activities for civic education tailored to the needs of all students, especially language learners. Brothers John and Hank Green's popular YouTube channel, Crash Course, provides excellent resources for learning languages through content.

Change #19: Immersive Learning Through Resources for Virtual Field Trips
Immersing students in new experiences creates an authentic communication gap that can provide incentives for language learning. Virtual museum field trips are now a popular way to engage language learners and draw them into learning through immersive and interactive environments, such as the Metropolitan Museum of Art's MetKids, a website where students can explore, engage, and ask questions about art in English and other languages. The Getty Museum in Los Angeles invites learners to create personalized remakes of artwork using supplies they have at home, with hilarious and thoughtful results.

Change #20: Multimodal Learning Resources
Multimedia resources to help students learn the four primary language skills (speaking, listening, reading, and writing) are readily available. For example, the American English website from the U.S. Department of State provides instructional resources for both learners and teachers through the exploration of the four skills. Additional resources include Randall's ESL Cyber Listening Lab, ESL Video, and Epic.

Fourth Trend: Learning With Artificial Intelligence

Artificial intelligence (AI) tools are becoming intelligent partners for learning. They are not merely tools to duplicate human thinking but can be used to engage in, supplement, and augment or enhance thinking (Anderson et al., 2018; Executive Office of the President, 2016).

Change #21: Intelligent Computer-Assisted Language Learning
There are now AI tools that use natural language processing to adapt to the way students learn and customize learning (Kannan & Munday, 2018). One early example is ALICE (Artificial Linguistic Internet Computer Entity) or Alicebot (Wallace, 2009). New and emerging AI that has the potential to support language learning includes Rumi Agent, developed by Ali Jafari and his team at the Indiana University-Purdue University Indianapolis CyberLab. The website explains that Rumi is a digital mentor as well as a "digital cool buddy" who "recommends learning activities, social connections," and so on. Rumi Agent can be embedded into a learning management system for use in the online language classroom.

Moving Forward

Elements of all these changes underlie the suggestions throughout this book for activities that teachers can use to engage students. When Rip Van Winkle woke up, he thought his world was "bewitched." The online learning environment, as we know it today, is described as an "open world" (Bonk, 2012). Although this description is less enchanting than Rip Van Winkle's, it describes a world of endless and never-ending possibilities.

Conclusion

This chapter provides a brief overview of several readily observable ways the online environment has transformed English language teaching and learning. More methods are already in place and developing on a constant basis, requiring immediate shifts in—as well as bountiful invitations for—new ways of teaching, learning, and thinking.

Links for all online resources mentioned in this chapter can be found on the companion site for this book (www.tesol.org/engageonline).

References

Anderson, J., Rainie, L., & Luchsinger, A. (2018, December 10). *Artificial intelligence and the future of humans*. Pew Research Center. http://www.pewinternet.org/2018/12/10/artificial-intelligence-and-the-future-of-humans

Blake, R. (2011). Current trends in online language learning. *Annual Review of Applied Linguistics, 31*, 19–35. https://doi.org/10.1017/S026719051100002X

Bonk, C. (2012). *The world is open: How web technology is revolutionizing education*. Wiley. https://doi.org/10.1002/9781118269381

Bonk, C. (2016). Keynote: What is the state of e-learning? Reflections on 30 ways learning is changing. *Journal of Open, Flexible and Distance Learning, 20*, 6–20. https://www.learntechlib.org/p/174229

Crystal, D. (2011). *Internet linguistics: A student's guide*. Routledge. https://doi.org/10.4324/9780203830901

Dörnyei, Z. (1994). Motivation and motivating in the foreign language classroom. *The Modern Language Journal, 78*(3), 273–284. https://doi.org/10.2307/330107

Executive Office of the President. (2016, October). *Preparing for the future of artificial intelligence*. National Science and Technology Council, Committee on Technology. https://obamawhitehouse.archives.gov/sites/default/files/whitehouse_files/microsites/ostp/NSTC/preparing_for_the_future_of_ai.pdf

Favilla, E. (2017, December 7). How the internet changed the way we write—and what to do about it. *The Guardian*. https://www.theguardian.com/technology/booksblog/2017/dec/07/internet-online-news-social-media-changes-language

Gee, J. P. (2003). *What video games have to teach us about learning and literacy*. Palgrave/Macmillan. https://doi.org/10.1145/950566.950595

Great Northern Catskills of Greene County. (n.d.). *Rip Van Winkle*. https://www.greatnortherncatskills.com/arts-culture/rip-van-winkle

Hodges, C., Moore, S., Lockee, B., Trust, T., & Bond, A. (2020, March 27). The difference between emergency remote teaching and online learning. *EDUCAUSE Review*. https://er.educause.edu/articles/2020/3/the-difference-between-emergency-remote-teaching-and-online-learning

Kannan, J., & Munday, P. (2018). New trends in second language learning and teaching through the lens of ICT, networked learning, and artificial intelligence. *Círculo de Lingüística Aplicada a la Comunicación, 76*, 13–30. https://doi.org/10.5209/CLAC.62495

Kenyon, C., & Hase, S. (2001). *Moving from andragogy to heutagogy in vocational education.* https://eric.ed.gov/?id=ED456279

Kramsch, C. (1993). *Concept and culture in language teaching.* Oxford University Press.

Moll, L. C., Amanti, C., Neff, D., & Gonzalez, N. (1992). Funds of knowledge for teaching: Using a qualitative approach to connect homes and classrooms. *Theory Into Practice, 31*(2), 132–141. http://www.jstor.org/stable/1476399

Pawan, F. (2017). Reflective pedagogy in online teaching. In F. Pawan, K. A. Wiechart, A. Warren, & J. Park, *Pedagogy & practice for online English language teacher education* (pp. 15–28). TESOL Press.

Wallace, R. S. (2009). The anatomy of A.L.I.C.E. In R. Epstein, G. Roberts, & G. Beber (Eds.), *Parsing the Turing test* (pp. 181–210). Springer. https://doi.org/10.1007/978-1-4020-6710-5_13

Weller, M. (2011). A pedagogy of abundance. *Spanish Journal of Pedagogy, 249*, 223–236. https://www.jstor.org/stable/23766391

CHAPTER 2

Actionable Principles for Engaging and Motivating Students in the Online Environment

By Faridah Pawan and Curt Bonk

This chapter focuses on principles for action as we work to motivate language learners engaging in the online medium, which include online presences principles, TEC-VARIETY online motivational principles, and English language learning approaches in online motivation.

Presences Principles in Teaching Online

The concept of presence is fundamental for understanding teaching in the online medium, and the community of inquiry (CoI) framework has been the guiding framework in online teaching and learning (Garrison et al., 2000). In the CoI framework, teaching, cognitive, and social presences are fundamental elements that guide the pedagogical perspectives in the medium. In addition to the original presences in the CoI framework, Shea and Bidjerano (2010, 2012) and Shea et al. (2014) have introduced the concept of learning presence. The four presences are used as the foundation for discussions in this book and can be understood in the following ways:

- Teaching presence is the design and facilitation of student engagement, as well as teacher-directed instruction in the online classroom.

- Cognitive presence is engagement in the online classroom that takes students through the stages of intellectual challenge and inquiry exploration, construction, integration, interrogation, and validation of ideas.

- Social presence is the extent to which students and teachers can project, while online, "realness" in their identity as a person, in the purpose of communication, and in building relationships with others.

- Learning presence includes "the attitudes, abilities, and behaviors that active and engaged students bring to their individual and collaborative online activities" (Shea et al., 2014, p. 10).

Although the presences overlap in the ways they are enacted and how they affect online learning and teaching, each presence is an identifiable entity on its own. These presences contextualize the various suggested teaching activities in this book to motivate online language learners. In the following section, we discuss Bonk and Khoo's (2014) actionable TEC-VARIETY framework of online motivation principles, which guide the design of these activities with the presences in mind.

Convergence of TEC-VARIETY Principles With Online Presences in Online Student Motivation

TEC-VARIETY's individual principles (table 2.1) constitute a framework that reflects an interplay of multiple factors of student motivation in the online medium (Bonk & Khoo, 2014). The enactment of these principles is most effective when they are taken into consideration and integrated into all teaching design and efforts.

Table 2.1. *Bonk and Khoo's TEC-VARIETY Principles*

Principle	Description
1. Tone	safety, comfort, sense of belonging
2. Encouragement	feedback, responsiveness, praise, support
3. Curiosity	surprise, intrigue, unknowns
4. Variety	novelty, fun, fantasy
5. Autonomy	choice, control, flexibility, opportunities
6. Relevance	meaningful, authentic, interesting
7. Interactivity	collaborative, team-based, community
8. Engagement	effort, involvement, investment
9. Tension	challenge, dissonance, controversy
10. Yielding products	goal driven, purposeful vision, ownership

Source: Bonk & Khoo (2014).

The tone (#1) and encouragement (#2) principles converge most clearly with elements of teaching and social presences (see chapters 4 and 6) in that they require teachers' direct engagement and express meaningful support through the engagement. Rather than using rewards and punishment, Bonk and Khoo (2014) stress the effect of external reinforcements provided by instructors on encouraging and promoting students' online motivation. These reinforcements can include timely, ongoing, and personalized feedback and assessments that can be adapted to students' abilities.

The setting's tension (#9), variety (#4), and relevance (#6) principles relate most closely to cognitive presence (see chapter 5). The thrust in these TEC-VARIETY principles is that learning is best achieved, and students are most motivated, when students experience challenges of desirable difficulty, such as solving problems without predetermined solutions and exploring authentic real-world tasks to construct understanding and meaning. These efforts can be undertaken on their own and in collaboration with others.

The principles of engagement (#8) and interactivity (#7) converge with the concepts of teaching and social presences (see chapters 4 and 6). Learning is a social process, and collaborative engagement with others is a core component in that process. To that end, learners need to see themselves personally, culturally, and linguistically included in online courses if they will be motivated to participate. Thus, online teaching must move toward inclusive instructional design (teaching presence)—that is, instruction that reflects and encompasses the "diversity of learner experiences, including differences in age, gender, cultural background, education, language, socioeconomic status, family and employment commitments, goals, objectives, needs, desires, and access to technology" (Gunawardena et al., 2018, p. 9).

Connections can be seen between students' sense of curiosity (principle #3) and autonomy (principle #5) and learning presence (see chapter 7). Within these connections, teachers foster students' abilities to be active seekers and processors of information and to self-plan, self-direct, self-regulate, and self-monitor their learning. The aim of all of these principles is the movement toward or attainment of processes and outcomes that encompass principle #10, yielding products that align with students' goals, vision, and sense of ownership.

The principles embedded in the TEC-VARIETY framework provide guidelines for motivating students when they are learning online. We see these principles as converging with the four online presences that guide the thinking in this book.

Saliency of English Language Teaching Approaches to Online Presences

In this section, we point out specifically the salient features in several English language teaching approaches as they relate to the four online presences. We include this section to reassure teachers that they can rely on their expertise in the field to undertake online instruction.

It is important to note here that teaching presence is a necessary component for each approach, as teachers are instrumental in designing, facilitating, and undertaking instruction across the board.

Communicative Language Teaching Approach

The most salient feature of the communicative language teaching approach (Chomsky, 1957) is the authenticity of the communication. The approach includes principles to motivate learners by engaging them in open-ended and meaningful communication (social and cognitive presences) and activities (i.e., task-based, problem-based, and content-based activities; cognitive presence) to the point that they feel compelled to use their second language, regardless of their level of proficiency or language background. This motivation only happens if the activities are authentic and have real-life extensions, or if there is additional authentic information needed or opinion gaps the learner wants to fill (social and learning presences). The activities focus on language use, not simply the accumulation of knowledge of the language. The activities also emphasize fluency and take accuracy into consideration whenever meaning is affected. (To learn more about communicative language teaching, visit www.professorjackrichards.com/wp-content/uploads/Richards-Communicative-Language.pdf.)

Community Language Learning Approach

The most salient features of the community language learning approach (Curran, 1976) are communal learning and the lowering of a language learner's anxiety. Topics of conversation are student generated, and members are expected to actively listen to each other as a means to connect in conversations in the target language (learning presence). The approach focuses on motivating students through working together in collaborative use of the target language (social presence). Rather than serving as authority figures, teachers are mentors and counselors whom students can seek should they need help (teaching presence). Teachers serve both to establish community and enhance the feeling of safety and security in learning in collaboration with other community members. (To learn more about the community language learning approach, visit iteslj.org/Articles/Koba-CLL.html.)

Content-Based Instruction Approach

In the content-based instruction approach (Brinton et al., 1989), the most salient feature is integration of language and content. Students are motivated to simultaneously sustain their language and content achievement (cognitive presence). Motivation is also evident in guiding students to perceive their second or foreign language as a means to think and learn. To achieve these goals, students are supported with content-obligatory language (i.e., required language for students to develop, master, and communicate, given the content material) and content-compatible language (i.e., the useful language for the concept being taught). Thus, language learning is highly contextualized in content, and ideally, ESL/EFL and content-area teachers work together to support their language learners (social presence). (To learn more about content-based instruction, see Richards, 2006.)

Lexical Approach

The most salient features of a lexical approach (Lewis, 1993) are authentic language recognition and production. The motivating element in this approach is engaging students to pay attention to large chunks of language as exemplars rather than spending time on the analyses of discrete grammar items (cognitive presence). The core of this approach involves helping students perceive and use natural patterns by first imitating them, then using them in new contexts; teachers should then guide students to find ways to use and customize the patterns in their language use. Learners can work with collections or corpora of the language of most frequently used expressions in identifiable combinations. The Corpus of Contemporary American English and the British National Corpus, for example, are two of the largest searchable databases that contain expressions in use that range from those in popular media to academic texts. (See a comparison of both at https://corpus.byu.edu/coca/compare-bnc.asp. To learn more about the lexical approach, see Guoxiang & Linlin, 2011.)

Natural Approach

Learning through comprehensible input is the most salient feature of the natural approach (Krashen & Terrell, 1983). Krashen and Terrell's conception of comprehensible input is important in motivation because it creates pathways for students to access meaning (cognitive presence). The first aim is for students to understand what they hear and read as they engage in interpersonal communication with others and in everyday language situations (e.g., conversations, shopping, listening to the radio; social presence). These pathways can involve teachers using multiple resources, such as information from students' home and cultural backgrounds, contextual information, gestures, multisensory forms of information (e.g., audio, pictorial, verbal, written), students' native languages, and peer and collaborative learning (learning presence). The input, however, is provided at a level of difficulty that is one step beyond students' proficiency level to encourage students to put in the effort and strive toward improvement (cognitive presence). (To learn more about comprehensible input, see TeacherVision, n.d.)

Sheltered Instruction

Scaffolded learning of language and content is the most salient feature of sheltered instruction (Echevarria et al., 2000). Learners are motivated in this approach by comprehensive scaffolding strategies so they can proceed autonomously with learning content taught in the second or foreign language (teaching presence). Specifically, teachers engage in intensive efforts to support students' learning in the following areas:

- Preparation (e.g., differentiating and setting language and content objectives)
- Instruction (e.g., building background, using comprehensible input, using multimodal resources strategically, interacting through first language collaboration, integrating all four skills in practice and application, and focusing on learner-centered approaches in lesson delivery)
- Review and assessment (e.g., providing an ongoing and comprehensive review of language and key concepts, providing timely and regular feedback, connecting comprehension to both languages and content objectives)

(To learn more about sheltered instruction, see Hansen-Thomas, 2008.)

Silent Way

The most salient feature of the silent way (Gattegno, 1983) is learning through solving puzzles. This approach may appeal to learners who see learning as a series of problems to be solved or, more specifically, as a process of solving puzzles (cognitive presence). In the silent way, teachers present students with charts that have small wooden or plastic colored Cuisenaire rods that represent different vocabulary, grammar points, or sentence structures. Students manipulate the rods as a means to understand their use in the language. Teachers remain mostly silent throughout this process to encourage learners to solve the puzzles and problems themselves. (To learn more about the silent way, see Shepherd, n.d.)

Suggestopedia

When implementing suggestopedia (Lozanov, 1978), the main salient feature is motivating learning through a relaxed state of mind. The main motivating element of this approach is lowering students' affective filter or their fear and anxiety, which can be achieved through a comfortable setting, a positive atmosphere in the classroom, and a trusting teacher-student relationship (social presence). In this approach, learning and retention are best achieved when students are relaxed. The use of soothing music sets the scene, and different parts of the music can be used to accompany different stages of classroom activities involving decoding of material, a concert session (e.g., active reading and listening), and elaboration of items for understanding (cognitive presence). Students and teachers relate to one another as audience members who enjoy an activity together, and teachers can often be seen reading aloud to students to the accompaniment of music. (To learn more about suggestopedia, see Bowen, n.d.)

Total Physical Response and Total Physical Response Storytelling

Motivating learning through physical activity and body language is the main feature of total physical response (TPR; Asher, 1969) and TPR Storytelling (Ray & Seely, 2004). Language learners are motivated through kinesthetic engagement in language learning. Students can be directed to use body movements, gestures, facial expressions, and other physical means to point to items, respond to commands, act out, express meanings, and so on as they engage in English language learning (learning presence). Teachers support these physical expressions and engagement through modeling. TPR Storytelling, an extension of TPR, contextualizes this engaging learning in high-interest stories that are told to students and then retold by the students using language supported by physical actions (cognitive presence). (To learn more about TPR and TPR Storytelling, see Fluency Fast, n.d.)

Translanguaging

Translanguaging (García, 2009) features learning through all languages in meaning construction. Students are motivated to engage through the use of all the languages they have at their disposal to communicate meaning and to comprehend (learning presence). In this regard, translanguaging is different from code-switching. The former is the learners' simultaneous and autonomous use of all language resources in meaning construction (cognitive presence), while the latter is a deliberate shift to another language to further enhance meaning or when the language in use is insufficient or unable to express the intended meaningfully (García, 2009).

Conclusion

This chapter has focused on principles that guide the online motivation strategies included in this book. We see online learning motivation as an ongoing process in the language classroom (Dörnyei, 2001), which we explore in the following chapters using the strategies described in this chapter. The presences (teaching, cognitive, social, and learning)—as well as the TEC-VARIETY motivational framework and an array of proven English language teaching principles and approaches—guide us in the journey.

Links for all online resources mentioned in this chapter can be found on the companion site for this book (www.tesol.org/engageonline).

References

Asher, J. J. (1969). The total physical response approach to second language learning. *The Modern Language Journal, 53*(1), 3–17. https://doi.org/10.2307/322091

Bonk, C. J., & Khoo, E. (2014). *Adding some TEC-variety: 100+ activities for motivating and retaining learners online.* Open World Books.

Bowen, T. (n.d.). *Teaching approaches: What is suggestopedia?* One Stop English. https://www.onestopenglish.com/methodology-the-world-of-elt/teaching-approaches-what-is-suggestopedia/146499.article

Brinton, D. M., Snow, M. A., & Wesche, M. B. (1989). *Content-based second language instruction.* Heinle & Heinle. https://doi.org/10.3998/mpub.8754

Chomsky, N. (1957). *Syntactic structures.* Mouton.

Curran, C. A. (1976). *Counseling-learning in second languages.* Apple River Press.

Dörnyei, Z. (2001). New themes and approaches in second language motivation research. *Annual Review of Applied Linguistics, 21*, 43–59. https://doi.org/10.1017/S0267190501000034

Echevarria, J., Vogt, M., & Short, D. J. (2000). *Making content comprehensible for English language learners: The SIOP model.* Allyn & Bacon.

Fluency Fast. (n.d.). *What is TPRS?* Fluency Fast. https://fluencyfast.com/about-us/what-is-tprs/

García, O. (2009). *Bilingual education in the 21st century: A global perspective.* Wiley-Blackwell. https://www.perlego.com/book/1008729/bilingual-education-in-the-21st-century-a-global-perspective-pdf?utm_source=google&utm_medium=cpc&gclid=Cj0KCQjwiNSLBhCPARIsAKNS4_e9qRyAK3DdksRVr7_sAfGEbLqacr9fYGet-QT4HZCFvdskKl_tgPkaArrxEALw_wcB

Garrison, D. R., Anderson, T., & Archer, W. (2000). Critical inquiry in a text-based environment: Computer conferencing in higher education. *The Internet and Higher Education, 2*, 87–105.

Gattegno, C. (1983). The silent way. In J. W. Oller Jr. & P. A. Richard-Amato (Eds.), *Methods that work* (pp. 72–78). Newborn House Publishers.

Gunawardena, C. N., Frechette, C., & Layne, L. (2018). *Culturally inclusive instructional design: A framework and guide for building online wisdom communities*. Routledge Taylor Francis. https://doi.org/10.4324/9781315439204

Guoxiang, D., & Linlin, J. (2011, May 27–29). *The lexical approach for language teaching based on the corpus language analysis*. 2011 IEEE 3rd International Conference on Communication Software and Networks, Xi'an, China. https://doi.org/10.1109/ICCSN.2011.6013922

Hansen-Thomas, H. (2008, summer). Sheltered instruction: Best practices for ELLs in the mainstream. *Kappa Delta Pi Record*, 165–169. https://doi.org/10.1080/00228958.2008.10516517

Krashen, S. D., & Terrell, T. D. (1983). *The natural approach: Language acquisition in the classroom*. Prentice Hall.

Lewis, M. (1993). *The lexical approach*. Language Teaching.

Lozanov, G. (1978). *Suggestology and outlines of suggestopedy*. Gordon and Breach Science. http://www.worldcat.org/oclc/57121915

Ray, B., & Seely, C. (2004). *Fluency through TPR Storytelling: Achieving real language acquisition in school* (4th ed.). Command Performance Language Institute, Blaine Ray Workshops. http://www.worldcat.org/oclc/918566130

Richards, J. C. (2006). *Communicative language teaching today*. Cambridge University Press.

Shea, P., & Bidjerano, T. (2010). Learning presence: Towards a theory of self-efficacy, self-regulation, and the development of a communities of inquiry in online and blended learning environments. *Computers & Education, 55*(4), 1721–1731. https://doi.org/10.1016/j.compedu.2010.07.017

Shea, P., & Bidjerano, T. (2012). Learning presence as a moderator in the community of inquiry model. *Computers & Education, 59*(2), 316–326. https://doi.org/10.1016/j.compedu.2012.01.011

Shea, P., Hayes, S., Uzuner-Smith, S., Gozza-Cohen, M., Vickers, J., & Bidjerano, T. (2014). Reconceptualizing the community of inquiry framework: An exploratory analysis. *The Internet and Higher Education, 23*(10), 9–17. https://doi.org/10.1016/j.iheduc.2014.05.002

Shepherd, S. (n.d.). *Rediscovering silent grammar*. TeachingEnglish. https://www.teachingenglish.org.uk/article/rediscovering-silent-grammar

TeacherVision. (n.d.). *What is comprehensible input for ELL students?* TeacherVision. https://www.teachervision.com/learning-disabilities-month/what-is-comprehensible-input-for-ell-students

CHAPTER 3

Online Language Teaching Competencies: A Combination of Pedagogical Knowledge and Skills

By Faridah Pawan

This chapter discusses online teachers' praxis, the combination of pedagogical knowledge and teaching skills (Freire, 1970). The chapter includes a comparison of TESOL's Technology Standards Framework with the Quality Matters Online Instructor Skills Set and a consideration of instructional design as a value-added knowledge and skill set.

The standards and benchmarks discussed in this chapter can serve as anchoring points for teachers to situate their current online teaching expertise and as a guide toward the next steps in their professional development. Instructional design (ID) is included for consideration because it can provide an avenue for teachers to develop new skills or enhance existing ones.

Online Teaching Competencies in TESOL's Technology Standards

Technology alone will not lead to effective online teaching in ways that motivate learners; the use of technology must be guided by teacherly thinking and reasoning (Johnson & Golombek, 2016). TESOL's Technology Standards Framework and the Quality Matters (QM) Online Instructor Skills Set provide teachers in the field with this needed guidance.

TESOL's Technology Standards for Language Teachers (see the appendix) were created in 2008 by a team led by Deborah Healey, TESOL's 2019–2020 president. The team stressed the standards were developed for "those who are teaching completely face to face, completely online, or a mix of the two" (Healey et al., 2008, p. 4). When we compare TESOL's Technology Standards Framework to the current QM (2016) Online Instructor Skills Set, we find similarities. Table 3.1 demonstrates the TESOL standards' alignment with QM at the macro level of TESOL's goals.

Table 3.1. *Alignment Between TESOL's Technology Standards Framework and the Quality Matters (QM) Online Instructor Skills Set*

TESOL's Technology Standards Framework	Quality Matters Online Instructor Skills Set
Goal 1: Language teachers acquire and maintain foundational knowledge and skills in technology for professional purposes.	**Institutional context:** The instructor understands the institutional context in which s/he teaches.
	Technologies: The instructor is knowledgeable about the technologies used in the online classroom.
Goal 2: Language teachers integrate pedagogical knowledge and skills with technology to enhance language teaching and learning.	**Pedagogy:** The instructor understands the pedagogical components of the online teaching and learning process.
	Instructional design: The instructor understands the instructional design requirements of an online course.
Goal 3: Language teachers apply technology in record-keeping, feedback, and assessment.	**Assessment:** The instructor is knowledgeable about various methods of measuring the success of the teaching and learning process in the online classroom.
Goal 4: Language teachers use technology to improve communication, collaboration, and efficiency.	**Social presence:** The instructor establishes a social presence and communicates effectively through writing and/or audio/video.

Sources: Healey et al. (2008); QM (2016).

The first similarity can be found in TESOL's standards in Goal 1 and QM's focus on teachers' acquisition and maintenance of technological knowledge and skills. However, to be useful, the knowledge must be grounded in teachers' understanding of the situation and setting in which they teach, a sociocultural perspective that underlies all TESOL standards and is explicitly expressed in QM's skills set.

In Goal 2, TESOL's standards are like those of QM in their joint emphasis of the enactment of the knowledge and skills in pedagogy, which in QM would occur specifically in the online setting. Within this TESOL goal, teachers should also undertake the design and management of language-learning activities. Likewise, in terms of the QM skills set, instructional design is a necessary component of the instructional skill set for online teachers.

The use of technology for record-keeping, feedback, and assessment is emphasized by both the TESOL Technology Standards Framework and QM's Online Instructor Skills Set. Specifically, this standard involves evaluating and using relevant technology and collecting relevant data for assessment.

The use of technology in the online setting for QM focuses on maintaining social presence (see chapter 6). Similarly, in TESOL's Technology Standards Framework (Goal 4), the presence is critical and applies specifically to teachers' ability to maintain effective communication and collaboration not only with students, but with all stakeholders, including teachers' peers, administrators, and students' families.

The comparison of TESOL's Technology Standards Framework with QM's Online Instructor Skills Set also brought to the fore ID as a value-added teachers' online teaching competency.

ID as a Component of TESOL Teachers' Online Skills Set

ID as a field creates an avenue and motivation for teachers' growth and development in online teaching. The experience of Tjaden-Glass (2020) is illustrative. She was a language instructor for about 13 years before she went on to pursue a degree in ID. Her presentation at the 2020 Virtual TESOL Convention demonstrated the following value-added knowledge and skills in ID that complement her competencies in TESOL:

1. Extends knowledge to design instruction across media, including face-to-face, artificial reality, hybrid, and fully online environments.

2. Extends understanding and evaluation of technology because it plays a significant role in the present time across media.

3. Contributes to the design of both materials and learning experiences in ways that are coherent and address the outcomes set by TESOL's teachers.

4. Extends advocacy for students, with an emphasis on accessibility to content, such as through the emphasis on Universal Design for Learning's (UDL) principles (CAST, 2018) and strategies as a component of designers' competencies.

5. Shares and strengthens the learner-centered pedagogical principles of communicative and situated language teaching approaches in TESOL because ID competencies also involve teaching approaches based on the principles that learning and knowledge construction are student-centered collaborative and social processes.

ID competencies can help teachers design "presences" as articulated in this book. They can provide teachers with structures and processes for design that support content instruction, ensure content remains challenging for students, and maintain and facilitate engagement to enable students to take ownership of their learning.

Conclusion

The concept of praxis explains that theory and practice inform each other. In this chapter, we see the interconnection demonstrated clearly in how both TESOL's Technology Standards Framework and QM's Online Instructor Skills Set inform as well as complement Tjaden-Glass's (2020) online teaching competencies and skills. Conversely, Tjaden-Glass's practices inform how the field can be transformed and continue to grow. Thus, praxis underlies the symbiotic and circular relationship between theory and effective online teaching practices.

Links for all online resources mentioned in this chapter can be found on the companion site for this book (www.tesol.org/engageonline).

References

CAST. (2018). *Universal Design for Learning Guidelines version 2.2.* http://udlguidelines.cast.org

Freire, P. (1970). *Pedagogy of the oppressed.* Seabury Press.

Healey, D., Hegelheimer, V., Hubbard, P., Iaoannu-Georgiou, S., Kessler, G., & Ware, P. (2008). *TESOL technology standards framework.* TESOL Press. https://doi.org/10.14705/rpnet.2016.eurocall2016.604

Johnson, K. E., & Golombek, P. R. (2016). *Mindful L2 teacher education: A sociocultural perspective on cultivating teachers' professional development.* Routledge Taylor Francis.

Quality Matters. (2016). *Online instructor skills set.* https://www.qualitymatters.org/qa-resources/rubric-standards/teaching-skills-set

Tjaden-Glass, S. (2020, July 18). *Instructional designer: An alternative career path for TESOL professionals* [Paper presentation]. TESOL 2020 Virtual Convention.

Appendix: TESOL Technology Standards for Language Teachers

Goal 1: Language teachers acquire and maintain foundational knowledge and skills in technology for professional purposes.

- **Standard 1:** Language teachers demonstrate knowledge and skills in basic technological concepts and operational competence, meeting or exceeding TESOL technology standards for students in whatever situation they teach.
- **Standard 2:** Language teachers demonstrate an understanding of a wide range of technology supports for language learning and options for using them in a given setting.
- **Standard 3:** Language teachers actively strive to expand their skill and knowledge base to evaluate, adopt, and adapt emerging technologies throughout their careers.
- **Standard 4:** Language teachers use technology in socially and culturally appropriate, legal, and ethical ways.

Goal 2: Language teachers integrate pedagogical knowledge and skills with technology to enhance language teaching and learning.

- **Standard 1:** Language teachers identify and evaluate technological resources and environments for suitability to their teaching context.
- **Standard 2:** Language teachers coherently integrate technology into their pedagogical approaches.
- **Standard 3:** Language teachers design and manage language learning activities and tasks using technology appropriately to meet curricular goals and objectives.
- **Standard 4:** Language teachers use relevant research findings to inform the planning of language learning activities and tasks that involve technology.

Goal 3: Language teachers apply technology in record-keeping, feedback, and assessment.

- **Standard 1:** Language teachers evaluate and implement relevant technology to aid in effective learner assessment.
- **Standard 2:** Language teachers use technological resources to collect and analyze information to enhance language instruction and learning.
- **Standard 3:** Language teachers evaluate the effectiveness of specific student uses of technology to enhance teaching and learning.

Goal 4: Language teachers use technology to improve communication, collaboration, and efficiency.

- **Standard 1:** Language teachers use communication technologies to maintain effective contact and collaboration with peers, students, administration, and other stakeholders.

- **Standard 2:** Language teachers regularly reflect on the intersection of professional practice and technological developments so that they can make informed decisions regarding the use of technology to support language learning and communication.

- **Standard 3:** Language teachers apply technology to improve efficiency in preparing for class, grading, and maintaining records.

Source: Healey et al. (2008), pp. 29–40.

PART II

The Ways to Engage Online Language Learners

CHAPTER 4

Teaching Presence and Engaging Students Through Teacher Self-Presentation, Course Design, and Facilitation

By Xiaojing Kou, Faridah Pawan, and Sharon Daley

Teaching online is an all-encompassing endeavor. In the online environment, the online teacher's role requires an ability to provide instruction as well as design and maintain an environment conducive to learning. This is the essence of the concept of teaching presence. This chapter discusses teaching presence and its connection to language learning motivation. It also provides suggested activities, tools, and scaffolding to enact teaching presence to motivate students through three elements: teachers' self-presentation as a trusted and safe entity, course design (first contact and course interface), and facilitation of engagement (synchronous and/or asynchronous).

Teaching Presence and Language Learning Motivation

Teaching presence involves structuring the learning environment so that when students enter it, they know where their teachers are leading them and how their teachers will support them. In the online environment, students must perceive teaching presence despite the fact that their teachers are not physically with them. In this case, teaching presence is a comprehensive concept with three central components that go beyond the instruction of content to include the design and facilitation of engagement structure so that learning can take place. In table 4.1, we provide an overview of the concept of teaching presence.

Table 4.1. *Teaching Presence:*

DIRECT INSTRUCTION: Providing intellectual and scholarly leadership	DESIGN AND ADMINISTRATION: Thinking through the process, structure, evaluation, and interaction components of the course	FACILITATING DISCOURSE: Supporting and encouraging participation toward the attainment of learning objectives
1. Present content. 2. Initiate questions. 3. Focus the discussion. 4. Confirm understanding through assessment and timely feedback. 5. Diagnose and address misconceptions. 6. Refer students to resources.	1. Build curriculum. 2. Customize (repurpose) materials (including online commentaries and personal insights). 3. Design and administer a mix of group and individual activities. 4. Set and negotiate timelines. 5. Provide guidelines and tips. 6. Model appropriate netiquette. 7. Model effective use of the medium. 8. Provide a sense of the "grand design" for the course (narrative paths could be used to make explicit and implicit learning goals apparent).	1. Comment on and encourage student responses. 2. Draw in less active participants. 3. Curtail effusive and dominating comments. 4. Help students find congruent linkages between opinions. 5. Assess the efficacy of the discussion process.

Source: Adapted from Anderson et al. (2001), pp. 1–17.

Teaching presence overlaps with cognitive presence (chapter 5) and social presence (chapter 6). Similar to the face-to-face context, in the online environment, effective teachers are those who can provide intellectual leadership, meaning they are knowledgeable about the content and know how to engage students cognitively in co-constructing and interrogating the content with them (cognitive presence). Teaching presence also overlaps with social presence (chapter 6) in that effective teachers are those who can connect with students affectively. In this chapter, however, we focus on the aspects of online teaching presence that involve teachers thinking deliberately and ahead of time and how to incorporate the two presences in the online environment.

Teaching presence is connected to the teacher-specific factors (Dörnyei, 1994, p. 280) for motivating second language learners and foreign language learners. First, the ways teachers project themselves, their teaching styles, and their preferences contribute to an environment in which students want to work hard so they can meet their teachers' expectations in favorable ways (affiliative motive). Second, students are motivated when they know what is expected of them and that they will be supported. This fact converges with teaching presence, which requires the teachers to design the online environment and facilitate engagement in it so students can understand the teacher's intent, efforts, and pathways to engage and include them.

In this chapter, we suggest activities for teachers to plan ahead of time, ways to make themselves a trusted and safe entity in the class community, ideas for the design of the classroom environment, and thoughts on how to structure engagement.

Part I: Online Learning Activities and Tools to Project the Teacher's Persona

Activity 1: Teacher Self-Storying Through Story Mapping
(Pawan et al., 2021)

Ages
Upper elementary through adult

Description and Purpose
Teachers have to take the lead in sharing information about themselves to create a safe and trusting environment for students to share their own information. Teachers need to find ways to express themselves so students can get to know who they are as individuals and as teachers.

Suggested Tool
ArcGIS

ArcGIS enables teachers to narrate who they are with pictures and maps. This storytelling tool provides students with a perspective of who they are in a visual and spatial sense. The maps enable teachers to situate themselves geographically and serve as invitations for students to do the same.

Scaffolding
Ms. Cleveland's Story Map provides one example from a teacher who agreed to share a story map to guide colleagues in creating their own. (The link for this resource can be found on the companion site for this book [www.tesol.org/engageonline].)

Activity 2: Multidimensioning the Teacher
(Pawan et al., 2021)

Ages
All

Description and Purpose
Just as teachers are interested in knowing their students, students are equally interested in who their teachers are because they are finding ways to relate to teachers as individuals. For teachers to share multiple aspects of themselves, we suggest that in addition to discussing the roles they play or hobbies they enjoy, teachers also include multiple short video clips of themselves in different locations, such as their office, their backyard, or a street they visited. They can also add images, photos, drawings, and presentation slides with audio voice-overs. If teachers are uncomfortable sharing real pictures of themselves, they can also use video animation tools such as Vyond or comic storyboard tools such as Storyboard That to illustrate interests and extracurricular activities.

Suggested Tools
Google Slides, Vyond, Storyboard That

Activity 3: Making Your "Grand Design" Transparent
(Pawan et al., 2021)

Ages
Upper elementary through adult

Description and Purpose
Teachers can express their thinking about how they plan to teach the class. Anderson et al. (2001) point to teachers sharing their thought processes as a means to including students as "co-conspirators" in classes, which teachers can achieve by projecting themselves this way. The teachers can provide this narrative in regular intervals throughout the online class.

Applications such as Voki enable teachers to create a speaking character to express their thinking. Here is a sample transcript of the description of Faridah Pawan's "grand design":

> In my classes, I alternate between direct instruction and discussion facilitation on our journey to work and learn from each other and to draw from the engagement what is most meaningful. What keeps me awake most nights is finding the right balance in my own participation/teacher presence in the class so that I do not get in the way.
>
> In any case, I may have gone a bit too long with my self-storying, but I wanted to share with you some of what I am thinking as an invitation for you to share with me some of your thoughts on how you plan to participate in class, difficulties you might have, and suggestions you have about how we can work together. Let's do it, team!

Teachers can also use applications such as Bitmoji to create personalized, playful cartoon avatars in ways that reflect who they are. They can use a Bitmoji on the welcome page for a Canvas course, in formal documents such as syllabi, in personalized feedback on students' work, and in class materials such as newsletters and posters.

Suggested Tools
Avatar Maker, Bitmoji, Voki

Activity 4: Meme-ing the Teacher
(Pawan et al., 2021)

Ages
Upper elementary through adult

Description and Purpose
As an alternative to using images or videos, teachers can also use memes or sayings borrowed from the internet. Memes can be from movies, television shows, comic books, photos, or drawings that demonstrate (often in humorous ways) certain ideas or personality characteristics teachers want to project about themselves. Teachers can also create these memes.

Suggested Tools
Meme Generator, quickmeme, MemeMarket, Make a Meme, Canva (meme generator)

Activity 5: Gamifying Introductions

Ages
All

Description and Purpose
Gaming activities offer a fun way for teachers to project themselves and build rapport with students in online language classes.

Suggested Tools and Games
Factile, Kahoot!, Gimkit, Quizizz, Two Truths and a Lie (game), Eight Nouns (game)

Scaffolding
Games played in face-to-face settings can be adapted for an online class to build active and lively self-introductions and course orientation. For example, on Kahoot!, Two Truths and a Lie can be a quiz-based game that allows teachers and students to write three statements about themselves, two of which should be true and one that should be a lie. After teacher modeling, teachers can mingle with students as they ask questions in smaller groups. On Google Slides, the game Eight Nouns can be played for introductions. Teachers and students post eight nouns that describe themselves, and the prompt should include directions to give a one- or two-sentence explanation of how each noun applies to the learner. The teacher needs to be one of the first people, if not the first, to post their eight nouns. Having the teacher go first or early allows students to get to know teachers and offers a model for any learners who are unclear about the expectations.

Activity 6: Creating Spaces in the Classroom to Be Present and Informal

Ages
All

Description and Purpose
Creating an informal space in the online class allows teachers to engage informally with students. Besides being another venue for teachers to share who they are with students, this informal space can let students know their teacher is approachable.

Suggested Tools
CourseNetworking (CN), YouTube, Kaltura My Media

CN can be incorporated into learning management systems (LMS) such as Canvas. CN has social media features such as allowing students to like a post. Teachers can create personal video channels with tools such as YouTube. Finally, teachers can create a media gallery of videos they recorded or uploaded to share informally through a private course channel in which both the teacher and the students can post and share videos.

Part II: Designing Students' Initial Experience (Teachers as Designers)

At the first opportunity to draw students' attention and set an approachable and purposeful tone for the class, teachers should keep in mind the following suggestions:

- Have the course site accessible to students a week or so before the first day of class so they can browse the course.
- Create a Start Here page to explain to students how to navigate the course site.
- Develop an introduction using ideas from the teacher self-projection activities in this chapter.
- Create warm-up activities that are engaging and serve a purpose. Create spaces for purposeful engagement, such as a discussion forum for students to ask questions about the class and their expectations.
- Ask students to record and share the pronunciation of their names and explain the meaning of their names if they choose. NameCoach can be used for such a purpose.

Course Interface Checkpoints

Description and Purpose

In online classes, the distance and sense of uncertainty about where to go for help make it critical to design students' first experience with the course well. The course interface can help students stay organized and motivated (or at least keep them from getting frustrated). Acknowledging the differences between course management systems, we limit our discussion and examples to Canvas, the LMS by Instructure. When creating an effective interface, we suggest teachers do the following:

- Use modules to serve as an organizer or compiler for all the activities for each week or each unit from various Canvas components (e.g., Discussions, Media, Assignments).
- Decide what items to enable (to facilitate access to content or activities) and what items to hide or disable (to minimize confusion) to simplify course navigation.
- Use guidelines from Universal Design for Learning to increase accessibility by making sure there are multiple means of representing information, multiple pathways for students to engage, and multimodal means for students to showcase their achievements.
- Use images in the public domain or ready-made templates. Teachers can search for images that have open-use licenses such as Creative Commons licenses (see fig. 4.1). When using images not in the public domain, instruction for how to give proper attribution can be found at creativecommons.org/use-remix/attribution.

Figure 4.1. Searching for images with Creative Commons licenses

Part III: Structuring Synchronous and Asynchronous Engagement (Teachers as Facilitators)

Description and Purpose

What is the optimal configuration of synchronicity and social space (individual, group, whole class) for an online language learning environment? Teachers can use the four quadrants (see fig. 4.2) as a tool to make decisions and map activities. Boxes with shade indicate when teachers are actively present.

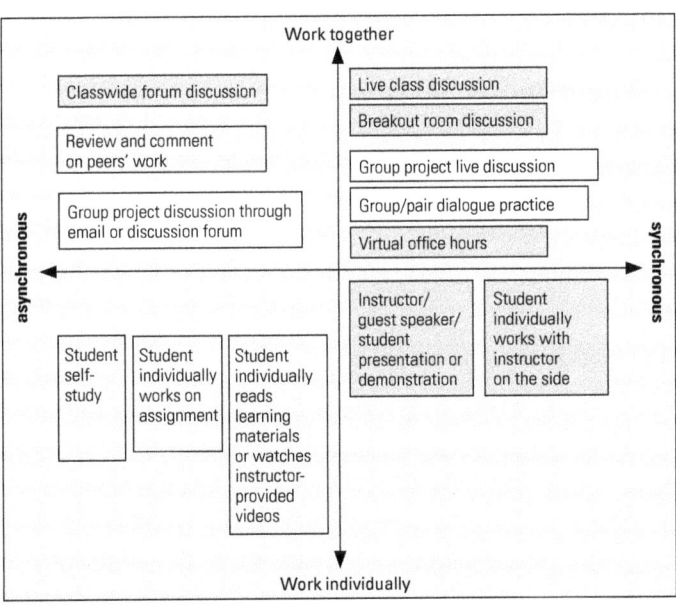

Figure 4.2. Mapping activities to synchronous and asynchronous social spaces in an online class

After mapping activities to synchronous or asynchronous sessions, the teacher should consider the following options:

- Use synchronous sessions when students need immediate access to teachers and asynchronous time for content that can be learned through individual consumption, construction, and reflection. For example, most grammar and vocabulary learning can be accomplished by students studying materials on their own.
- Provide more synchronous time for learners with lower levels of autonomy.
- Use asynchronous forums for discussions that require in-depth reflection and deliberation.
- Use asynchronous activities to provide frequent, low-risk formative assessment and increase learner-content interactivity to make up for the lack of synchronous time.
- Use a combination of synchronous and asynchronous features to engage students in different types of learning communities (e.g., a classwide learning community fostered by asynchronous activities, such as a discussion board; synchronous or asynchronous activities involving smaller groups or pairs of students, such as critical friends, language partner, group work).
- Use a combination of synchronous and asynchronous modes to create ample opportunities for students to learn from each other and connect with the teacher (e.g., discussion forum, Facebook, Twitter, TikTok, CN).
- Use an asynchronous system of reminders and frequent feedback to add a sense of synchronicity when students are learning on their own.

Scaffolding Synchronous Sessions

At the beginning of a synchronous session, teachers can support and motivate students in the following ways:

- Open the online space at least five minutes before the scheduled start time.
- Play music. Students will understand that once the music ends, it is time to get started.
- Reward or engage early arrivals.
- Engage students in a warm-up activity (e.g., free writing for three minutes).
- Live chat with students. Develop a bank of routine questions to ask.
- Play a language game (see resources in chapter 1, Change #14).
- Engage students in non-language activities (e.g., free online Zumba and yoga activities).

During a synchronous session, teachers can support and motivate students in the following ways:

- Print out an attendance roster and record student participation to have a visual aid to help determine which students need encouragement to participate.
- Use think-aloud and read-aloud activities to make teacher thinking transparent.
- Assign roles for breakout room discussions (e.g., note taker, task manager, group spokesperson).
- Provide a clear template for engagement (e.g., key phrases to use in discussions).
- Create reflection and meditation time for students to think before responding; embed quick, low-stakes assessments (e.g., short quizzes, quick polls, or a Quizlet game); and create pathways for synchronous check-ins with the teacher (e.g., combining PowerPoint slides with a predesignated column [adopting the "two content" layout] and the annotation tool in Zoom, which allows students to annotate on the slide at the same time the teacher shares the PowerPoint slides in an online class [see fig. 4.3]).

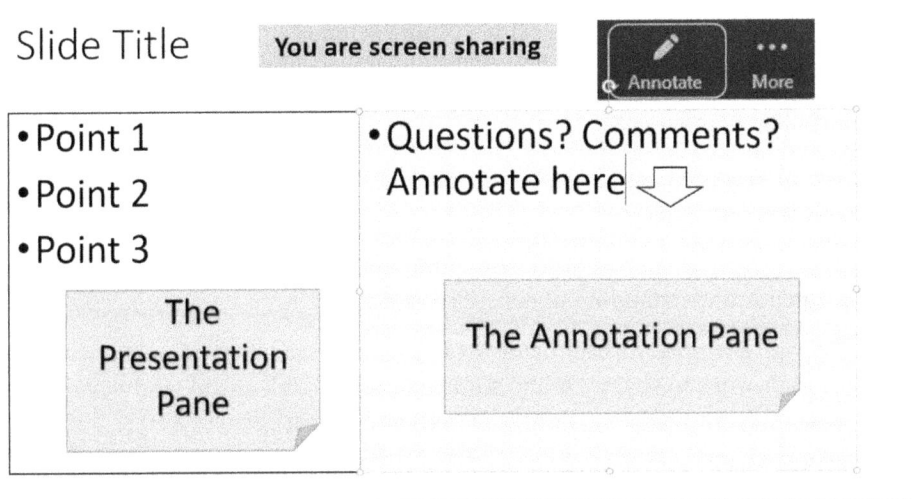

Figure 4.3. Example of PowerPoint slide with predesigned layout for live annotation by students

For the end of synchronous sessions, teachers should institute routines to signal the end of the class and engage students in the following ways:

- Invite students to share their one "muddiest point" (on which they need more clarification and help from the teacher) through the chat function.
- Allow students to linger and socialize informally.

Scaffolding in Asynchronous Sessions

When teachers decide to implement asynchronous instruction, they can support and motivate students in the following ways:

- Set a routine for sending out announcements to help students organize their time. Multiple and random announcements are overwhelming and easily ignored.
- Maintain interaction by limiting the length of postings (100–300 words). However, encourage students to post as often as they like.
- Develop clear roles and responsibilities for students to participate.
- Have students self-code their participation (e.g., indicate their discussion roles).
- Provide a timeline with benchmarks for the completion of specific portions of a project.

Whether using synchronous or asynchronous instruction, teachers can put supports in place that will help create teaching presence and guide students, both of which will contribute to students' motivation. Teachers can use the following methods:

- Create recorded assignment explanations and mini-lessons that clarify challenging concepts.
- Use teacher-developed videos or commercially available videos to support students' understanding of course content.
- Provide exemplary assignments from previous students, or create new examples of their work to share. Online students like to work ahead, and having these examples allows them to proceed at their own pace.
- Create varied and supplementary support to increase the comprehensibility of input (e.g., provide visual cues that include illustrations, manipulatives, images of real-life objects, diagrams, and drawings. Google Street View or infographic maker templates in Canva are two examples.).
- Provide shareable living documents or resources. These help students reach out to classmates and the teacher for help (e.g., Google Docs and the digital wall Padlet). Figure 4.4 shows a screenshot of a weekly digital wall created with Padlet where the class can work together to document and share learning experiences and resources. The screenshot shows three columns—Weekly Goals

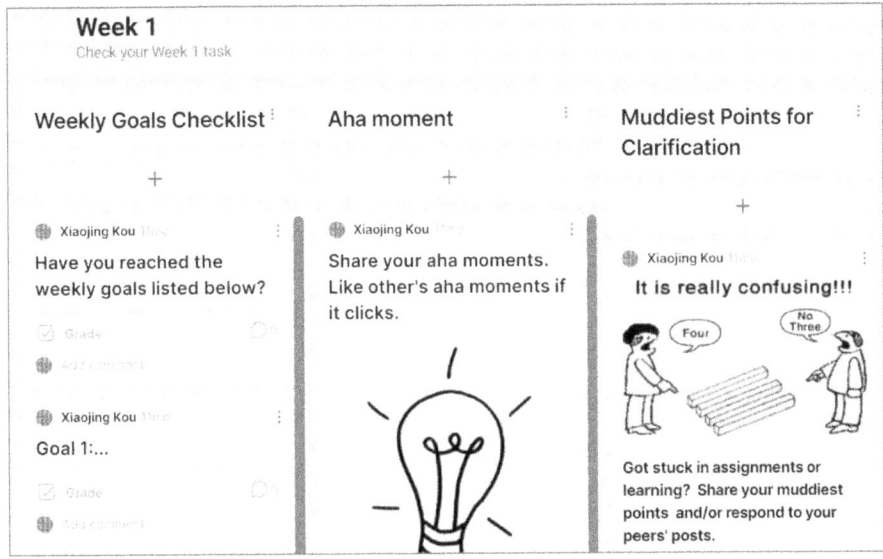

Figure 4.4. Example of a Padlet digital wall

Checklist, Aha Moment, and Muddiest Points for Clarification—but it can include more columns, such as Helpful Resources, I Need Help, Learning Tips, and Social Corner. (To see the full example on Padlet, visit bit.ly/week1padlet.)

Conclusion

In this chapter, we offer tools, activities, and processes teachers can use to develop teaching presence in their online language learning environments. When teachers are thoughtful about establishing teaching presence, students will relate to them and become autonomous learners. The ideas in this chapter focus on helping teachers provide effective instruction by designing and maintaining an environment in which students can learn.

Links for all online resources mentioned in this chapter can be found on the companion site for this book (www.tesol.org/engageonline).

References

Anderson, T., Rourke, L., Garrison, D. R., & Archer, W. (2001). Assessing teaching presence in a computer conferencing context. *Journal of Asynchronous Learning Networks, 5*(2) 157–172. http://dx.doi.org/10.24059/olj.v5i2.1875

Bonk, C. J., & Khoo, E. (2014). *Adding some TEC-variety: 100+ activities for motivating and retaining learners online.* Open World Books.

Dörnyei, Z. (1994). Motivation and motivating in the foreign language classroom. *Modern Language Journal, 78,* 273–284. https://doi.org/10.2307/330107

Pawan, F., Lankford, A., Li, Z., Pollard, K., Yan, Y., & Zhou, J. (2021). *Culturally and linguistically inclusive online teaching* [Course module, Governor's Emergency Education Relief Fund Project]. Indiana University.

CHAPTER 5

Cognitive Presence and Engaging Students Through Challenge and Higher-Order Thinking

By Faridah Pawan and Sharon Daley

Unless the online environment is managed well, there can be a prevalence of "serial monologues" (Henri, 1991), which is defined as one-way communication in which students are engaged only at the beginning levels of Bloom's taxonomy (Conklin, 2005). This chapter on cognitive presence focuses on finding ways to motivate students through activities that move them toward critical and higher-order thinking. Garrison et al. (2001) define cognitive presence as when students engage online with peers and instructors alike, in a back-and-forth process of constructing and reconstructing experiences and knowledge through "the critical analysis of the subject matter, questioning, and challenging assumptions" (p. 7).

This chapter discusses the connection between cognitive presence and student motivation in language learning and provides suggested activities, tools, and scaffolding to enact cognitive presence and engage learners.

Connection Between Cognitive Presence and Student Motivation in Language Learning

Cognitive presence is an invitation for students to engage online in meaningful ways, using the affordances of the medium. Forms of engagement include being able to reflect on ideas shared and stored online to capitalize on the internet's "open world" (Bonk, 2009) access to resources, learn anything at any time, and collaborate with those near and far. In language learning, this type of engagement occurs when students experience a challenge with "desirable difficulty" (Bjork & Bjork, cited in Mercer & Dörnyei, 2020, p. 129). Ideally, this challenge involves engaging students in activities they find difficult to do on their own but can undertake with teachers' or peers' support and guidance.

Garrison et al. (2001) developed the Practical Inquiry Model, which reflects four cyclical phases of critical thinking and cognitive presence:

- *Initiation phase*, which includes a triggering event that begins the dialogue about a particular issue
- *Exploration phase*, in which students move from private reflection to social exploration and exchange information about the issue at hand with others
- *Integration phase*, when participants begin to co-construct meanings or solutions to the issue using the ideas explored in the previous phase
- *Resolution phase*, in which the proposed solution is "vicariously tested," individually or with others, in a new context or a new way

In the following section, we suggest activities that are designed to promote cognitive presence in online language learning and include guidance for how to scaffold the activities for students of various ages.

Suggested Online Learning Activities, Tools, and Scaffolding Approaches

The types of activities we describe and suggest in this section engage students in inquiry, reflective thinking, construction and reconstruction of ideas, problem-solving, and the use of multiple perspectives in collaboration with peers and teachers alike.

Activity 1: Inquiring and Collaborating by Creating and Immersing in Roles

Ages
Upper elementary through adult

Description and Purpose
Online discussions that lead to collaboration and inquiry can be challenging to achieve. Discussion forums in any learning management system can be used to enact cognitive presence discussions. Teachers can assign and develop specific as well as intriguing roles, or the students can develop the roles themselves. The roles should give structure to the discussions so students know ways to engage and demonstrate how their contributions can connect with those of others (and help teachers monitor students' participation).

Suggested Online Discussion Roles
An overarching framework for three main types of roles can be derived from Pawan et al. (2017) and made evident through the instructions provided to students:

- *Starters:* Students in this role are the first to post questions and raise themes from the prompts or readings.

- *Provocateur:* Students with this role ask questions or share contrary additional evidence or information.
- *Wrapper:* In this role, students summarize and add thoughts or questions to the discussions, including additional resources for future reference.

Scaffolding

- Students can self-code the discussion roles and types of postings. This metacognitive strategy will help students keep track of their responses.
- Modify or use roles within high-preparation, ongoing, and low-preparation discussion strategies. Teachers can use "The Big List of Class Discussion Strategies" by Jennifer Gonzalez (www.cultofpedagogy.com/speaking-listening-techniques). Teachers can use high-preparation strategies such as a gallery walk, in which students share and talk about their projects on VoiceThread, or backchannels (e.g., maintaining chat conversations in tandem with Zoom discussions in ongoing strategies); teachers could also have students create opinion posters in low-preparation strategies such as affinity mapping.
- Students can create roles for themselves. Curt Bonk (2009) has a series of roles he has developed over the years that could be modified by students or used as a basis for students to develop their own roles (see table 5.1).

Table 5.1. *Bonk's Discussion Roles Sampler*

- Reflector/Thinker/Speculator/Observer/Watcher
- Warrior/Debater/Arguer/Conqueror/Bloodletter
- Idea Squelcher/Biased/Preconceiver
- Artist/Idea Person/Muse
- Energizer/Inventor/Generator/Brainstormer
- Adventurer/Discoverer/Explorer/Armchair Travel Agent
- Controller/Executive Director/CEO/Leader
- Connector/Realtor/Linker/Synthesizer
- Decider/Judge/Settler
- Devil's Advocate/Critic/Censor

Source: Bonk (2009).

Activity 2: Self-Reflecting and Reflecting With Critical Friends

Ages
All

Description and Purpose
The ongoing nature of these types of reflections allows online language learners to revisit their understanding. When teachers provide opportunities for online language learners to reflect with critical friends (peers whom learners can rely on for support, either informally or formally) on their language learning, create a representation of their learning, justify the understanding of the course content, and compare their new learning at various points, they engage students in higher-order thinking.

Suggested Tools
Prezi, Loom, GoReact, WhatsApp, Bubbl.us, Mindomo, Text2MindMap

When using Prezi or similar resources, teachers can choose from a wide variety of simple tools that help students create interactive graphic organizers. After the instructor has created supportive materials for each activity in Loom or GoReact, teachers can create higher-order thinking prompts for reflections, such as analysis (e.g., How does this concept change your thinking about this?), synthesis (e.g., In what ways do these ideas connect?), or evaluation (e.g., What is missing from the idea, in your opinion?).

Prezi allows students at all levels to graphically represent the connections between various concepts, easily revise the representation as they reflect on the changes in their thinking, include multimedia links and other images, and more. This reflection activity works best when it focuses on overarching concepts rather than discrete skills. In Prezi, the students can share their work with the teacher for comments, as well as to help other students.

Loom allows online language learners to create and share artifacts. For example, in writing instruction, Loom allows students to record their screen while narrating their writing process. GoReact enables learners to obtain feedback from their teacher and peers in terms of the way they are physically using the target language. Students video-record themselves to capture their formal "performance" (e.g., presentation) or how they use the language in real practice (e.g., in informal conversation). Teachers and critical friends can provide timely feedback on the videos.

WhatsApp messages can be used for individual or collaborative reflections about readings or so students can ask for help. Bonk and Khoo (2014) label these types of activities as the "muddiest points" reflection activity, which will "help learners review key points and summarize the content, which the instructor can then check for understanding" (p. 77).

Scaffolding
When engaging students in reflection, whether self-reflection or with critical friends, teachers should be clear about their expectations. One way to support learners as they reflect is to provide prompts to guide the reflection (e.g., How does your new learning connect to what you already know?). They can also model their own reflection process in writing or in an audio- or video-recorded think aloud.

Activity 3: Going Into Action Through Art Immersions and Remakes

Ages
All

Description and Purpose
Students are often most engaged when they can choose objects to experience and learn about, manipulate the artifacts, or engage in the creation of new artifacts to share with others. Online virtual tours of museums provide students with such opportunities by enabling them to interact with the art in meaningful ways that go beyond passive viewing.

Suggested Websites and Tools

- World museum tours, such as the Uffizi Gallery tour (a partner of the Google Arts and Culture initiative), Louvre virtual tour, and the National Gallery of Art
- Google Arts and Culture initiative (artsandculture.google.com), an online platform on which students can search for high-resolution images and videos of artwork and cultural artifacts from more than 2,000 partner museums, including the Museum of Modern Art, the British Museum, the Palace Museum in China, and National Museum in New Delhi
- Discipline-specific museum tours. For those interested in archaeology and anthropology, Bonk and Khoo (2014) recommend the Smithsonian National Museum of Natural History, which has narrated tours to see interactive online displays of bones and skeletons of animals.
- Children's Museum Indianapolis, which has interactive displays for children in its Children's Museum Indianapolis at Home program
- J. Paul Getty Museum and remakes of great artworks. Students can modify a favorite artwork to their liking based on art in the museum's virtual gallery, using home appliances, friends, pets, or anything they have available to them. Examples of the remakes can be seen at blogs.getty.edu/iris/getty-artworks-recreated-with-household-items-by-creative-geniuses-the-world-over.

Scaffolding
Teachers can introduce these activities by recording and making available a guided tour of the sites to support young or beginning students. Teachers can offer students the choice of attending and asking questions at a live tour session, which can be conducted in the students' first language. Teachers can also enlist students to create a rubric for choosing and evaluating artwork. Another way to support all learners is to create options to help students process and remember the museum experience, such as having them create a story based on the artwork or research to explain the intention of the artist or even the interpretations that have been given to the piece. For younger learners, ChatterPix can provide a multimodal and personal way to continue engagement with the art: Students take a picture of the artwork and add a voice to animate the characters in the artwork, and classmates can then respond.

Activity 4: Socializing the Process of Writing

Ages
Upper elementary to adult

Description and Purpose
Writing is a social process—a recursive and never-ending process of drafting, reviewing, editing, and revising with others. Responses from peers help writers improve their texts, but the process of reviewing itself engages everyone in critical analysis and inquiry.

Suggested Tools
We suggest teachers use the following three applications together to support each step of the writing process (see table 5.2), as they are useful for walking students through a process that is both public and private. These applications are mostly available on a learning management system such as Canvas and through other online services (e.g., WordPress, Wikidot, Google Sites).

- Asynchronous forums can be a starting point for students to brainstorm ideas with each other. The ideas and discussions saved in the forum also serve as a place students can revisit as they proceed.
- Personal reflections on the writing can be shared via a blog to enable teachers and peers to see the thinking behind students' ideas.
- Students and their peers can use a wiki jointly to develop and refine ideas before writing is published.

Table 5.2. *Writing Process Using Forums, Blogs, and Wikis*

Forums (collaborative)	Blogs (individual)	Wikis (collaborative)
Identifying requirements and resources; discussing goals and intended audience; brainstorming ideas	Sharing reflections about the writing artifact, thought process	Developing drafts of the writing that incorporate revisions and suggestions; selecting a final version of drafts for submission or public sharing

Scaffolding
The discussion forums can be a place for hard scaffolding (Saye & Brush, 2002) in that they can be a repository for instructions, rubrics, and supporting materials such as existing examples, as well as a place for questions and answers. Additionally, the archived versions on wikis enable students to see how their ideas and those of others helped their writing evolve. Teachers can provide dynamic, timely, and ongoing support by using the blogs as a place to identify students' struggles, which they can address individually and directly (Saye & Brush, 2002).

Activity 5: Problem-Solving and WebQuesting

Ages
Upper elementary through adult

Description and Purpose
Teachers can develop or help students generate authentic problems for the latter to demonstrate both their ability to understand the process of problem-solving and the ability to actually solve problems. The problems are authentic to the extent that they may reflect real-life dilemmas or engage students in solving problems that do not have predetermined solutions. Students are engaged as they use resources and ingenuity in collaboration with peers to solve problems.

Suggested Problem-Based Lesson Repositories
Bernie Dodge (2021) created the original template and repository of WebQuests or inquiry- and problem-based lessons (see webquest.org). Contemporary examples of English language learning and second and foreign language WebQuests, for different levels of proficiency and age groups, can be found at Nellie Muller's ESL WebQuests, TeachersFirst, Education World, and QuestGarden.

Scaffolding
Scaffolding steps are built into the creation of WebQuest lessons and include the following:

- *"Ill-defined" problem:* Students are presented with the unsolved problem or mystery (e.g., the King Tut WebQuest at www.margietyner.net/king-tut-webquest.html).
- *Tasks:* Students are directed to explore the various sources, evidence, and suspects.
- *Process through roles:* Students are given individual roles in a group to assume as a guide in their research and so they can participate and collaborate to solve the problem.
- *Resources:* Students receive information and process resources, including how to collaborate and undertake multimodal presentations.
- *Evaluation and conclusion:* Students use rubrics as a guide, a means to track their progress, and a support to understand teachers' expectations.
- *Teacher pages:* These are available to help fellow teachers use already created WebQuests.

Activity 6: Engaging in Culture Through Stories and Folktales

Ages
All

Description and Purpose
Stories and folktales enable students to delve into each other's culture in a more contextualized way and beyond the surface level of the "5 Fs" of culture (food, festivals, famous people, flags, and fashion). The stories and folktales are distanced from the students and not personally revealing, but they provide in-depth insight into a culture. The activities we share here have the potential to involve students in online conversations and dialogues about daily realities, choices, reasoning, and circumstances that are important to people in stories and folktales. This activity offers a different but more critical way of seeing and learning about other students' cultures in a language class.

Suggested Tools
Padlet, Google Slides, Kleki, ReadWriteThink, Google Translate, Magnetic Poetry

The online language learning environment affords opportunities for multimodal scaffolding of critical responses to stories and folktales. When using Padlet, teachers can create a digital board where students can publish stories from their countries of origin and that could include values that may be difficult for outsiders to understand. Inviting students to share and comment on these stories on a Padlet enables them to start conversations that can continue and get more in depth, as well as branch out into other language and literacy projects.

Kleki is an online painting tool that enables the user to create a digital piece of art as a response to stories and folktales. Students can also respond to these stories using ReadWriteThink's Venn Diagram tool, which enables students to compare and contrast versions of stories and visualize the similarities and differences in their components.

Magnetic Poetry is a web app that enables students to write poems as one of the response choices. This app activates students' cognitive presence because they are creating something new based on their learning.

Scaffolding
The online learning environment allows learners to engage with folktales uniquely because they have access to multiple versions of a specific folktale, multimodal versions of the folktales, and information on the history of the folktale. Using the built-in features in Google Slides, students can collaborate to summarize and synthesize the story. Students can use Google Translate to provide the story in its original language, along with the English or translated version for a critical evaluation.

Activity 7: Exploring Current Events

Ages
Middle school through adult

Description and Purpose
Streaming media and the increase in participatory online news have created a lot of content to understand and digest for both enjoyment and critical appraisal. The following activities aim to engage students in both synchronous and asynchronous discussions through informal and formal means.

Suggested Tools
Teleparty, LiteMap, Word Lens, online glossaries

Teachers and students can watch movies and television series together on Netflix. The Teleparty feature adds a group chat function so students can watch together and discuss the movie or show at the same time. Teachers can join in to respond to questions. Students can be each other's discussants and informants as they watch the show. The added features of subtitles and closed captioning can be used to support students' learning.

Bonk and Khoo (2014) point to Cohere (now LiteMap) to engage students collaboratively in undertaking coherent and organized debates using ideas they can locate through public and private tagging systems. LiteMap includes access to feeds from multiple news sources, blogs, and social networking sources, and students can use all of these to make their overall structure and thinking about their arguments explicit in ways that will strengthen their arguments as they prepare to debate the opposing side.

Scaffolding
Although the news should be delivered at a language level that is accessible to a broad range of individuals, scaffolding could be offered in a couple of ways:

- Word Lens is a tool that translates printed words instantly using a video camera. The same capability is available on many cell phones.

- Students can use interactive multimedia glossaries and language corpora to help them understand words and phrases in context. Tools include the Corpus of Contemporary American English (www.english-corpora.org/coca) and the British National Corpus (www.natcorp.ox.ac.uk), each of which offers robust and comprehensive collections of words from at least eight genres, including from spoken texts, fiction, popular magazines, newspapers, academic texts, movie subtitles, blogs, and other webpages.

Conclusion

This chapter focuses on finding ways to engage students in activities that help them enact cognitive presence. The ideas in the chapter aim to motivate students through the challenge of engagement in activities requiring critical and higher-order thinking.

Links for all online resources mentioned in this chapter can be found on the companion site for this book (www.tesol.org/engageonline).

References

Bonk, C. J. (2009). *The world is open: How web technology is revolutionizing education.* Wiley.

Bonk, C., & Khoo, E. (2014). *Adding some TEC-VARIETY: 100+ activities for motivating and retaining learners online.* OpenWorldBooks.

Conklin, J. (2005). Untitled. [Review of the book *A taxonomy for learning, teaching, and assessing: A revision of Bloom's taxonomy of educational objectives, complete edition*, by L. W. Anderson, D. Krathwohl, P. Airasian, K. A. Cruikshank, R. E. Mayer, P. Pintrich, J. Raths, & M. C. Wittrock]. *Educational Horizons, 83*(3), 154–159. https://www.jstor.org/stable/42926529

Dodge, B. (2021, October 23). *Welcome.* Webquest. https://webquest.org/

Garrison, D. R., Anderson, T., & Archer, W. (2001). Critical thinking, cognitive presence and computer conferencing in distance education. *American Journal of Distance Education, 15*(1), 7–23. https://doi.org/10.1080/08923640109527071

Henri, F. (1991). Distance learning and computer-mediated communication: Interactive, quasi-interactive or monologue? In C. O'Malley (Ed.), *Computer supported collaborative learning* (pp. 145–161). Springer. https://doi.org/10.1007/978-3-642-85098-1_8

Mercer, S., & Dörnyei, Z. (2020). *Engaging students in contemporary classrooms.* Cambridge University Press.

Pawan, F., Wiechert, K. A., Warren, A. N., & Park, J. (2017). *Pedagogy and practice for online English language teacher education.* TESOL Press.

Saye, J., & Brush, T. (2002). Scaffolding critical reasoning about history and social issues in multimedia-supported learning environments. *Educational Technology Research & Development, 50*(3), 77–96. https://doi.org/10.1007/BF02505026

CHAPTER 6

Social Presence and Engaging Students Through Community

By Sharon Daley, Faridah Pawan, and Xiaojing Kou

Media that use video conferencing and enhanced visual support create the ideal environment for enacting social presence in the online language classroom. Social presence and teaching presence intersect in setting an educational climate that is trusting, respectful, and encouraging of openness in the classroom, which supports a collaborative construction of knowledge and skills.

In this chapter, we discuss the connection between social presence and student motivation in language learning and suggest activities, tools, and scaffolding to enact social presence and engage learners.

Connection Between Social Presence and Language Learner Motivation

Social presence refers to the genuine and real connections students can make with their community members (peers and the teacher), as well as their ability to project themselves socially and affectively (Rourke et al., 2001).

Social presence has a special significance in an online language class. The effectiveness of the presence has a direct connection to the affective domain of language learning. In the domain, the emphasis is on creating an environment in which students can overcome anxiety (Henter, 2014). Teachers and students can alleviate anxiety through the creation of a safe, open, fun, and—most importantly—authentic communicative environment. Creating this type of environment is particularly important because language learners often communicate using what they know and what is familiar to them, especially in the beginning stages. When practicing the target language, students are more likely to talk about their daily life, preferences, family, and culture in a safe and authentic environment.

In that sense, teachers' enactment of social presence may take place as part of their efforts to motivate students to use language communicatively and purposefully and to feel comfortable doing so. In a class that focuses on the communicative approach, for example, without students feeling connected or invited to actively engage or that the engagement has a meaningful purpose, the class cannot proceed (Richards, 2006). Although grammatical accuracy can play a role, the focus of a communicative class is on fluency or students' ability to express, exchange, and understand ideas meaningfully through genuine and real social interactions. In such a class, teachers' central role involves enacting and supporting students' social presence—that is, creating learning situations in which students can practice connectiveness and purposefulness in using language to interact online.

Online Learning Activities, Tools, and Scaffolding Approaches

Activity 1: Creating Communal Spaces

Ages
Middle school through adult

Description and Purpose
To establish a sense of belonging and community in a classroom, students must have a place in the class where there is enculturation, meaning that all students, regardless of their proficiency levels or experiences in the class, can share stories, examples, and experiences. This space must also enable students to stay on the periphery of engagement, if they choose to do so, but still be able to learn from the experiences of their classmates. These spaces can serve as virtual "hanging out spaces" to motivate learners to connect; use their developing target language skills with a supportive, nonjudgmental audience; and extend the online language learning community beyond the bounds of the current members of the class.

Suggested Tools
Chat tool in learning management system (LMS), chat tool in Zoom, Facebook, Twitter, Instagram, LinkedIn

Scaffolding
Teachers can scaffold these communal spaces by encouraging students to informally greet each other, meet up, or ask each other or the teacher questions. This sense of community can be expanded beyond the bounds of the current members of the class by creating a Course Fan Page (Bonk & Khoo, 2014, p. 60) to motivate learners to interact outside of the course assignments and activities, which can, in turn, strengthen the bonds between students. These bonds can create avenues of support that will motivate learners to persevere in their learning if they encounter challenges. A Course Fan Page can also motivate online language learners to create networks that endure after the completion of the course. In an online language learning course, this type of engagement can allow language learners more robust and authentic opportunities to engage in the target language in an environment where their peers can support them.

Activity 2: Creating Opportunities for Mediated and Authentic Learning Through Pen Pals

Ages
Middle school through adult

Description and Purpose
The online medium enables learners to have informal and authentic communication with others. By having online pen pals, students can connect with fellow language learners or native speakers of the target language, no matter where they are located. In this activity, students can be guided toward creating a safe and authentic social space outside the limits of a formal class.

Suggested Tools
ePals, Students of the World, My Language Exchange, PenPal World, Flipgrid

Scaffolding
There are many ways to set up this activity to take advantage of an online language learning environment. The online language learning environment allows learners to go beyond written communication between pen pals. Students can use video creation tools such as Flipgrid to record messages for their pen pals. These tools give learners an authentic opportunity to create meaningful spoken messages for an audience outside the online classroom. These short videos can be exchanged with the pen pals through the course LMS, which allows the teacher access to the recordings in case they want to assess the students' learning, whether formally or informally. This type of pen pal exchange also affords students more immediate and frequent interactions with their pen pals, thus increasing the number of opportunities to practice their speaking and listening skills. These frequent interactions increase the number of instances in which learners can bring forth their social presence in the online learning environment.

In this activity, teachers will likely need to offer scaffolding according to the age and language level of the students in the online class. Students can work in groups to create their communications to their pen pals. Working in groups will allow the students to get feedback on their messages before sending them to their pen pals. Additionally, teachers can invite students to share with their classmates what they learned from their pen pals, connecting the local learning community with the outside social space.

Activity 3: Expanding Learning With Family at Home in a Virtual Books and Blanket Night

Ages
All

Description and Purpose
Teachers can create social presence by developing activities that use applications to facilitate "home-school connections" and allow students to engage others at home in using the target language for communication and enjoyment. The activities have the added benefit of family members being able to join in the language learning as well. In

the Books and Blanket Night activity, students can engage their parents in reading books together. Alternatively, teachers can invite families to a virtual space to listen to the teachers reading their favorite stories (Pawan et al., 2021).

Suggested Tools and Websites

- *Freechildrenstories.com (K–12):* This platform provides meaningful stories for children of all ages, and users can browse stories by age or style.

- *Epic! (K–6):* This web-based resource provides educators free access to thousands of books loved by kids in kindergarten through sixth grade.

- *Bookshare (K–12):* Bookshare is an online library of accessible ebooks to support learners with reading barriers, such as those with dyslexia, blindness, and cerebral palsy. The site helps learners customize their experience to suit their learning style and find books virtually that they need for school or work or just to enjoy.

- *Amrita Learning (K–12):* This site promotes engaging games and family learning. Their newest project in production targets customizable K–5 family literacy development, provides materials appropriate for all ages, and has scaffolded curriculum from kindergarten through fifth grade.

- *Extended Family "Teleparty":* The Teleparty application is a Chrome extension that is now a part of Netflix, Hulu, Disney Plus, and HBO and is available to those who have subscriptions to these streaming services and reliable servers. Using Teleparty, extended family members in different locations and with varying levels of target-language proficiency can watch movies together, have conversations about the movies, and help each other understand the movie.

Scaffolding

- *Bilingual resources (K–12):* Teachers can also provide bilingual and multilingual resources to help family members read with students. For example, Audible offers stories in six different languages that children can access using a computer, phone, or tablet.

- *Read Conmigo (K–5):* This site offers free children's books in English and Spanish. Learners and their parents can read these creative and engaging stories aloud together. The site provides helpful resources for children in preschool through fifth grade.

- *Discussion protocol (K–12):* When students watch media together with family members or classmates, sensitive and difficult issues may arise. We suggest teachers have available or provide families with conversation protocols that include guidelines for students to respect others' views. The protocols also create room for students to speak and be heard without interruption. The small-group discussion protocol shared by Endicott College (see this book's companion site) provides 20 examples of online conversation protocols.

Activity 4: Connecting With Real-World Experts

Ages
All

Description and Purpose
The online medium has not only enabled communication across time and space but also made the world "flat" (Friedman, 2005), meaning that students can connect with not only peers but also with "more knowledgeable others" (Johnson & Golombek, 2016). This activity invites teachers to bring outside facilitators, experts, and parents into the classroom. Teachers can enhance topics of discussion by engaging these visitors as knowledgeable and experienced individuals in the field or as audience members; the discussion can result in a classroom project. Engaging students and supporting them in the real and purposeful use of language can help teachers enact social presence.

Suggested Tools
Discord, Slack, Zoom

Scaffolding
Students can engage directly and safely with each other and with their guests in online communication. The teachers can create a specific channel for the visit that allows them to write comments to students while the guest is speaking, which is similar to using online "backchanneling" to scaffold students' learning. These comments can help teachers become aware of how students bring together information they learned in previous lessons or activities. These written conversations can be archived so they are available after the expert visits for teachers and students to review.

Activity 5: Creating a Sense of Community by Having Fun Together

Ages
All

Description and Purpose
Bonk and Khoo (2014) emphasize the importance of variety and fun in online instruction (and any educational setting) so activities can foster social interaction, extensive communication, and student engagement. In language learning, having fun together lowers learners' affective filters by creating a relaxing setting and positive atmosphere. Language games can integrate fun in meaningful communicative exchanges (Reinders & Wattana, 2011). Meaningful interaction further fosters social connectedness (Laffey et al., 2006) to strengthen social presence in the learning community. Gee (2005) sees games as capable of promoting deep learning, particularly if they can do the following:

- Engage students in authentic and meaningful communication that requires them to actively listen to and interpret their language partners' input.
- Encourage the participation of all parties (including those who are watching the students playing the game) by asking them to support and assist the players.

- Create interaction by providing feedback and possibly creating new problems for students to solve beyond the games.
- Provide the meanings of vocabulary words in a contextualized and situated manner.
- Prioritize and allow performance before competence so learners focus on engagement rather than worrying about their language proficiency.
- Engage students in risk-taking in pleasantly frustrating ways—learners feel their efforts pay off when they complete challenging but doable tasks.

Suggested Games
See chapter 1, Change #14, for resources for games, including the *Lost Words of Atlantis*, ESL Games World, Educandy, and ESL Games Plus.

Scaffolding
When first introduced to new games, learners need support for playing the game in the target language. One scaffold teachers can provide for learners to play the game in the target language is to model clearly how this game should be played. When the game is complicated, a video recording demonstrating how the game is played can be shared with students so they can watch it on their own. Teachers can also provide language support by including "subtitles" for the demonstration video. Basic language support includes providing key grammar patterns to use in the conversation and a possible vocabulary list. The teacher can ask students to reflect on the linguistic strategies used in the demonstration.

Activity 6: Creating a Community by Being Makers Together

Ages
All

Description and Purpose
The maker movement involves learning by doing. The connected nature of the online medium enables learners to live up to the movement's essence—the joy of making and sharing artifacts with others. By creating artifacts together, students engage in authentic communication and find ways to communicate and share ideas with others.

Suggested Websites and Tools
- *Web-based Inquiry Science Environment (WISE):* WISE is a free and open website that enables K–12 students to work together to do science with the support of integrated tools.
- *Storyjumper:* Students can create digital, interactive stories, poetry books, comic adventures, and more in multiple languages.

Scaffolding
The strategy Role, Audience, Format, and Topic (RAFT; Tomlinson, 2017) is a great way for teachers to undertake scaffolding and differentiation for maker projects by

listing role choices on a grid that can be created with multiple online tools for student collaboration. Table 6.1 shows Pawan et al.'s (2021) example of a RAFT cooking show lesson for middle and high schoolers. (More roles, audiences, formats, and topics can be included as needed.) Students can choose a row (or mix and match in some cases) for the final project to showcase their learning; the lesson provides students with the flexibility to complete tasks that fit their ability level and demonstrate their specific strengths.

Table 6.1. *Role, Audience, Format, and Topic (RAFT) Cooking Show Lesson*

Role	Audience	Format	Topic
Host	Team members	Write an interactive script.	What is our favorite cookie?
Cook	Students and teachers in class	Make a digital poster of a recipe.	How can we make the cookie?
Camera person	General public	Create a video.	Why should you try our cookie?

Activity 7: Connecting Through Curating Digital Albums

Ages
All

Description and Purpose
When students take a class online in their own space and spend a lot of time there, teachers can design ways for students to bring experiences from their own space to the communal space to share. Because the class is online, what students share can be revisited and reflected on several times.

Like a class yearbook, a digital album activity can bring students together by creating a sense of shared experiences. Students' diverse backgrounds and their interpretations of experiences their class has had together are valuable resources for teachers to tap into to engage students.

Suggested Tools
Google Slides, Pressbooks, Google Docs, Seesaw

Scaffolding
When creating a class album, teachers can invite students to collaborate with classmates to remind them of shared experiences. Teachers can encourage students to share an object or a written artifact or short piece of writing from class (e.g., poems, short stories, articles), then invite classmates to share what they remember about these artifacts or writings. Each student then gets a slide and adds their content to it (Google Slides allows learners to insert a wide variety of media elements). The completed album will display work by all students in one presentation and will be a combination of students' contributions and their classmates' memories.

Activity 8: Creating Pathways for Students to Celebrate Their Identity With Classmates

Ages
All

Description and Purpose
To help teachers and students get to know each other, teachers can design an activity related to students' names. Because people's names can bear the strongest connection to their identity and individuality—and, for English language learners, to their culture and community—names have enormous significance and can generate engaging discussions. Teachers can use ideas from books about names, such as *The Name Jar*, by Yangsook Choi; *Your Name Is a Song*, by Jamilah Thompkins-Bigelow; *My Name Is Sangoel*, by Karen Lynn Williams and Khadra Mohammed; or *Whoever You Are*, by Mem Fox (Pawan et al., 2021). Stories about names can also be used to create digital posters for a virtual gallery walk.

Suggested Tools and Websites
PicCollage, International Children's Digital Library, StoryWeaver

Scaffolding
Teachers should model the activity with their own names and provide guiding questions to help students think about the significance of names, including how to pronounce them correctly so their meanings come across as intended by parents or whoever selected the names. Using Name Coach features on an LMS can enable students to vocalize their names and preferred pronunciation.

Conclusion

In this chapter, we describe the importance of social presence for engaging students in learning languages online. To enact the presence, we focus on finding ways to develop a communicative environment that is open and welcoming to encourage and motivate interaction among students while also creating a sense of community in the class.

Links for all online resources mentioned in this chapter can be found on the companion site for this book (www.tesol.org/engageonline).

References

Bonk, C., & Khoo, E. (2014). *Adding some TEC-VARIETY: 100+ activities for motivating and retaining learners online.* Open World Books.

Friedman, T. L. (2005). *The world is flat: A brief history of the twenty-first century.* Farrar, Straus and Giroux. http://www.worldcat.org/oclc/57202171

Garrison, D. R., Anderson, T., & Archer, W. (2000). Critical inquiry in a text-based environment: Computer conferencing in higher education. *The Internet and Higher Education, 2*(2–3), 87–105.

Gee, J. P. (2005). *Good video games + good learning: Collected essays on video games, learning and literacy.* P. Lang. https://www.peterlang.com/document/1054442

Henter, R. (2014). Affective factors involved in learning a foreign language. *Procedia-Social and Behavioral Sciences, 127,* 373–378. https://doi.org/10.1016/j.sbspro.2014.03.274

Johnson, K. E., & Golombek, P. R. (2016). *Mindful L2 teacher education: A sociocultural perspective on cultivating teachers' professional development.* Routledge Taylor Francis. https://doi.org/10.4324/9781315641447

Laffey, J., Lin, G., & Lin, Y. (2006). Assessing social ability in online learning environments. *Journal of Interactive Learning Research, 17*(2), 163–177. https://www.learntechlib.org/primary/p/5981/

Pawan, F., Lankford, A., Li, Z., Pollard, K., Yan, Y., & Zhou, J. (2021). *Culturally and linguistically inclusive online teaching* [Course module, Governor's Emergency Education Relief Fund Project]. Indiana University.

Reinders, H., & Wattana, S. (2011). Learn English or die: The effects of digital games on interaction and willingness to communicate in a foreign language. *Digital Culture & Education, 3,* 3–29.

Richards, J. C. (2006). *Communicative language teaching today.* Cambridge University Press.

Rourke, L., Anderson, T., Garrison, D. R., & Archer, W. (2001). Assessing social presence in asynchronous, text-based computer conferencing. *Journal of Distance Education, 14*(2) 51–70. https://www.learntechlib.org/p/92000/

Tomlinson, C. A. (2017). *How to differentiate instruction in academically diverse classrooms* (3rd ed.). Association for Supervision and Curriculum Development.

CHAPTER 7

Learning Presence and Engaging Students Through Self-Directed Learning

By Faridah Pawan, Sharon Daley, and Xiaojing Kou

The online medium requires students to take ownership of their learning and be independent, self-motivating, and self-directed (Pool et al., 2017). Self-regulation and autonomy, which define online learning presence, have been studied extensively in the field of English language teaching and are fundamental in language learning motivation.

This chapter discusses the connection between learning presence and language learning motivation and suggests activities, tools, and scaffolding to enact learning presence and engage learners.

Four categories were structured by Shea et al. (2013) to capture learning presence in online learning experience: forethought and planning, monitoring, strategy use, and reflection (see table 7.1).

The concept of learning presence has direct connections to learner self-regulation and autonomous concepts, which are key motivational factors in language learning. There are two perspectives on autonomous learning. Holec's (1981) theory of autonomous learners defines autonomy as "the ability to take charge of one's own learning" (p. 3). Murray (2014) stresses that autonomy in language learning is a social construct. It is within a social context, where the learners interact with others, where autonomy emerges (Little, 2001). In both conceptualizations, teachers must draw out and create environments that enable learners to self-regulate and self-direct their language learning.

Table 7.1. *Learning Presence*

Category	Learner behavior
Forethought and planning	- *Goal setting:* Learner will decide on specific actions and outcomes. - *Planning:* Learner will decide on methods or strategies appropriate for the task. - *Coordinating tasks:* Learner will distribute and sequence subtasks to others or self for future completion.
Monitoring	- *Check for understanding:* Learner will seek verification of understanding of task, events, or processes. - *Identify problems:* Learner will identify difficulties or problems that interfere with completion of tasks, performances, products, or other outcomes. - *Noting completion:* Learner will make comments that indicate certain tasks or activities have been finished to support attaining a goal. - *Evaluating quality:* Learner will evaluate the quality of a product, its content, or its parts as working toward completion. - *Taking corrective action:* Learner will make statements that monitor individual or group performance that results in corrective action based on feedback or reflection. - *Appraising engagement:* Learner will comment about self or others' engagement, interest, commitment, or participation (includes personal reactions to tasks, materials, and activities). - *Recognizing learning behaviors:* Learner will make statements about individual or group preferences, strengths, or weaknesses as learners. - *Advocating effort:* Learner will encourage others to contribute or focus on interest, commitment, or participation (includes personal reactions to tasks, materials, and activities). - *Noting use of strategies:* Learner will make statements that illustrate they are mindful and aware of the strategies they are using.
Strategy use	- *Seeking or offering help:* Learner will request, offer, or provide assistance related to learning materials, tasks, processes, or products. - *Recognizing knowledge gap:* Learner will make statements indicating they are aware of a gap in knowledge and its connection to the current task, process, or product. - *Reviewing:* Learner will make comments noting the need to review or the completion of reviewing content related to the course. - *Noting outcomes:* Learner will make statements in which they acknowledge the relevance of current tasks or processes to a future outcome. - *Seeking and offering information:* Learner will look beyond course content and materials to locate additional information to deepen understanding.
Reflection	- *Change in thinking:* Learner will make statements that indicate a change in thinking as a result of process, product, or outcome. - *Causal attribution:* Learner will make statements in which they credit their results to their performance (e.g., use of forethought, planning, monitoring, strategies).

Source: Adapted from Shea et al. (2013).

Online Learning Activities, Tools, and Scaffolding Approaches

Activity 1: Self-Selecting Online Texts

Ages
All

Description and Purpose
Reading is one of the four domains of language, so providing learners with a choice in the texts they read can increase their motivation to engage in language learning. Simply providing learners with unlimited choice, however, is not sufficient to achieve this goal. Teachers need to teach learners how to self-select texts at levels they can read independently or with some help from the instructors.

In general, learners need to be able to independently decode between 95 percent and 98 percent of the words in a text to comprehend what they read.

Suggested Tools
Readworks, Newsela

Both tools include a range of topics to engage and motivate a wide variety of learners, as well as a broad continuum of levels in the texts. They allow learners to access topics of interest that also fit within their current reading levels.

Scaffolding

- *Beginners (levels 1 and 2):* Synchronously, via videoconferencing, a teacher can meet with the learner to demonstrate the process and provide in-time feedback regarding learners' decoding and how to determine their levels independently. Asynchronously, the teacher can record and post a video explaining and demonstrating the technique; after watching the video, learners can record themselves reading a text they have determined they can read independently or with some help from the teacher. The teacher can watch the video and provide feedback on the learners' determination of the text.

- *Secondary and adult learners:* Synchronously, through peer interaction, two learners read the same passage (or passages about the same topic but at varying levels of difficulty) and have a conversation about the text. Asynchronously, to assess the learners' decoding and fluency, the teacher can watch a video (or listen to an audio recording) of learners reading aloud and assess their reading using a multidimensional rubric (e.g., Rasinski's, n.d., Multidimensional Fluency Rubric Chart) and provide feedback to learners. Rasinski's rubric will allow teachers to provide students with an evaluation of their use of the components of fluent oral reading. Teachers can assess students' decoding through learners' written summaries on Google Doc and other interactive platforms.

Activity 2: Social Bookmarking and Annotation for Self-Directed Reading and Social Learning

Ages
Middle school through adult

Description and Purpose
In addition to giving students more control over what they read, teachers can provide a means for students to express reasons and preferences for what they read. They can share not only their reading choices but also their thoughts about what they read, so reading becomes a social process of active curation, sharing, and interaction with peers and ultimately builds one's own domain of knowledge and expertise. This activity integrates self-directed learning with social learning under a teacher's guidance.

Suggested Tools
Diigo, Scoop.it, Hypothes.is, Wakelet

We focus on Diigo's functionalities, as they apply to the other tools in general as well. First, readers can bookmark and save the bookmarks online. They can choose the words to tag the readings and organize them in multiple and personally meaningful ways. Second, readers can annotate an article by highlighting and adding notes to a web page. This feature turns a passive reader consuming content into an active and critical reader, note taker, commenter, and strategic user. Third, Diigo allows learners to create both private and public groups where group members can be notified when an article is bookmarked and annotated. Within a group, members can share bookmarks and annotations and "like" or comment on a shared article. In this way, readers are not reading alone. Finally, over time, saved bookmarks, user-created tagging systems, and user-added annotations can form a library that reflects a learner's identity as a learner, an explorer, a member of various Diigo communities, or even an expert in certain fields.

Scaffolding
Teachers can scaffold by providing support for students to choose the articles they read:

- *List of identified web-based articles:* For example, from a list of 10 articles identified by the teacher, learners choose five to read based on their own interest.

- *Particular site that is a collection of online readings:* For example, Kiwi Kids News has news articles on various topics that are safe, relevant, and fun. Students can then either read five articles on one topic (e.g., politics) or five articles on three different topics (politics, health, and science).

- *Particular topic to focus on:* Have learners search on their own and choose several articles.

- *Encouragement of social reading:* Teachers can group students, and each group member can choose their own reading, do their own annotation by highlighting and adding notes, and share their annotation in the group. Group members can also read each other's annotations and make comments. In the groups, learning presence can be further enhanced with a reflection activity in which each learner can reflect on the following points:

- Why is this the article I have annotated the most among all of the articles?
- What tags did I choose and why?
- How do annotations in this article help me reach the learning goals for reading this article?
- What is the purpose of the notes (e.g., provide definitions of unfamiliar words, add my thoughts, add an explanation to a point, pose a question)?

Activity 3: Badging for Self-Assessing and Creative Self-Rewarding

Ages
All

Description and Purpose
Shea et al. (2013) established the importance of online learners monitoring their own abilities and achievement levels (see table 7.1). When learners can award badges to themselves, they can demonstrate forethought by setting goals to earn certain badges (see fig. 7.1 for badge examples; Shea et al., 2013). They use forethought to establish a goal for themselves and make decisions about their actions in the learning community that will lead to the outcomes they desire. These behaviors can lead to the learners reflecting on their own learning. Learners can earn badges by demonstrating knowledge and skills they developed before entering the learning community, which can motivate

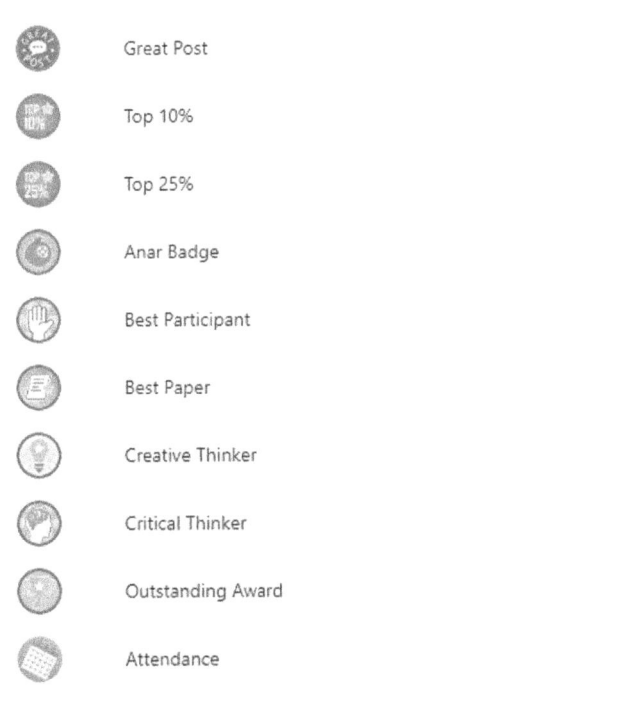

Figure 7.1. Examples of ready-to-use course badges

the learner to consider the knowledge and skills they bring to the online community and serve as an informal assessment so the teacher can determine what the learners bring with them to the experiences.

Suggested Tools
Badgr, Credly, CourseNetworking (CN)

According to its website, Badgr provides "skills-aligned digital credentials, stackable learning pathways, and portable learner records," while Credly is a badging tool educators can use to award badges designating accomplishments. Digital badges can be embedded in a system. For example, CN has a badging system with some existing badges, as well as a way for teachers to upload badges created for the course.

Scaffolding
To support learners who are new to badging, teachers could provide guidance in choosing a graphic that clearly represents an achievement and writing an explanation so learners understand the purpose of the badge. In this online badging system, teachers can help learners create an anonymous "identity" to mitigate the competitiveness of badging. At the same time, this feature can encourage creativity and a sense of whimsy when learners create these identities. Allowing learners to choose humorous avatars and nicknames to accompany their identity can encourage them to bring their own personalities, cultural backgrounds, and interests to this identity creation.

Activity 4: Photovoicing Through Instant Messaging

Ages
Upper elementary through adult

Description and Purpose
Photovoice is a process in which learners can use photographs to record and share events, activities, and phenomena in their community; engage in dialogue about those events and how they affect learners directly; and communicate about events, activities, and phenomena directly to decision-makers (Wang & Burris, 1997). Learners use devices with cameras to record and share events with others in their online circle of friends and beyond (see fig. 7.2).

Suggested Tools
WhatsApp, WeChat, LINE, Snapchat, Discord, Skype, Facebook Messenger

All of the listed instant messaging tools are compatible with photovoice projects because they enable learners to self-direct their participation in using language and the online medium to communicate and share their lived experiences immediately in authentic ways. The projects are also motivating in that learners participate actively as invested commentators of events surrounding them, rather than being passive bystanders, with the use of the devices and artifacts they have.

Scaffolding
Scaffolding photovoice projects is important, as these projects can be challenging on two fronts. First, learners may be unsure as to the types of pictures they should take.

Note: Picture taken by S. I. and shared with permission

Hello everyone! This is my photo, in this picture you see an old table, three empty dishes and a burning candle.

The old table: I remember when I was crying in an old table like this.

Three empty dishes: One day in the morning, I only had for breakfast three empty dishes, my children came to me, to tell me they were very hungry and the water didn't fill them.

The burning candle: At night in the darkness without lights because I could no pay for power. A person very important to me said me. Why aren't you studying? You can do it, you're a young and smart woman. And now I think that education can take me from darkness to light.

Figure 7.2. Photovoice project photograph and transcript: From darkness to light

Second, depending on language development levels, learners may need help with the type of descriptors and language resources they can draw from to describe the photos they captured. The example below provides the steps we undertook to implement photovoice in an English as a foreign language project in Costa Rica.

- *Step 1 (focusing project):* Teachers should provide a focus for the project. In this example, we identified the following title for our learners: "People, objects, and experiences that are important to me as I learn English."

- *Step 2 (helping learners describe using words):* We had several Google Classroom lessons using words and expressions to describe experiences. Our guiding prompts included, for example, describing the place and location; people's ages, actions, roles, and feelings; and learners' opinions of what they saw.

- *Step 3 (using bilingual samples from the teacher):* Photovoice projects are developed by using authentic and often personal examples. Invitations for this project should always start with examples from the teacher.

Figure 7.2 shares a Costa Rican learner's photovoice project, which was shared on WhatsApp, along with the transcript of how the learner described the photo.

Activity 5: Video Annotating

Ages
Upper elementary through adult

Description and Purpose: Motivation Through Visually Self-Monitoring Development

Creating and annotating video recordings of their own learning requires online language learners to "evaluate the quality of a product, its content . . . as students work toward completion" (Shea & Bidjerano, 2010). Learners record themselves performing an assigned task, such as reading a text in the target language or speaking about a recent personal experience. They then annotate the recording, pointing out their own (or others') strengths and areas needing improvement, as well as areas where they need assistance from the teacher.

Suggested Tools
GoReact, Edthena, VideoAnt

GoReact and Edthena are paid platforms that offer easy-to-use tools for sharing videos, annotating with time stamps, and providing the teacher with the ability to share supplemental documents with online learners. These paid platforms also offer online support for learners who experience technical issues. VideoAnt is the University of Minnesota's free video annotation platform (a basic version of the paid platforms).

Scaffolding

- *Video examples:* Teachers can use past learners' videos as support for current learners who are still uncertain about how the project should be done.

- *Rubric:* If using these video annotation platforms for a formal assessment, teachers can include a rubric to communicate the criteria used to assess the performance. Teachers can rely on WIDA's "Can Do" statements and descriptors when creating rubrics for online language learners. A rubric could also be created to evaluate written annotations if the project will be used to assess development of the target language in writing.

- *Peer review:* Teachers can extend online learners' experience with video annotation by including peer review in the process, which allows learners to engage with and help peers via their annotations.

Activity 6: Wikipedia Article Entries

Ages
High school through adult

Description and Purpose
The blurred distinction between the classroom and the outside world in the online medium gives both the teacher and the students easy access to the real world while they engage in learning (Benson, 2007; Allwright, 1988). Having students create article entries on wikis on topics they select is one way to bring together the classroom and the outside world. Publicly hosted wiki sites have a real audience and a community that actively reviews and edits the entries. These features provide the added benefit for students to see and learn from how they can develop and improve their contributions. Alternatively, wikis on those sites provide an opportunity for students to collaborate in editing or writing content. Needless to say, writing and editing publicly can be an intimidating task unless there is teacher support. Thus, teachers can also make use of wikis available in the learning management systems used in their own classes, such as Moodle and Blackboard. Teachers can then make the wiki entries viewable and editable by the students.

Suggested Tools
Wikipedia and other Wikimedia family members (e.g., Wikibooks and Wikinews), PBworks EDUHub, wikidot.com, Moodle, Blackboard

Scaffolding

- *Accounts:* If using publicly available wiki hosting services, students can create their own accounts. However, teachers can help by creating a public course account for their students to use.

- *Wikipedia writing support:* Teachers can use—and direct students to use—guidelines provided by Wikipedia.

- *Collaborative writing:* Students can write wiki articles in groups rather than individually.

- *Existing examples:* Instead of creating a new entry, students can choose their topics, then review a Wikipedia article to see if they can make further edits to elaborate on a certain topic. This revision can also be done by groups instead of individual learners.

- *Drafts:* Students do not have to start with writing or editing on the Wikipedia platform directly. Tools such as Google Docs can be used to finalize the draft before it is transferred to Wikipedia, if students prefer that method.

Activity 7: Student-Led Tools and Strategies Sharing

Ages
Upper elementary through adult

Description and Purpose
In this straightforward activity, students share with peers what tools they use to learn and how they use them. This activity directly addresses the metacognitive domain of learning presence (Shea & Bidjerano, 2010), especially in terms of strategy use, and enables learner voice and choice (Brooks & Young, 2011; Cook-Sather, 2006), two core mechanisms for motivating students.

Scaffolding
One approach teachers can take is to first model sharing language learning strategies with students. Several websites, such as FluentU and Babbel, have examples and references teachers can use.

Activity 8: Assessing Through Language ePortfolios

Ages
All

Description and Purpose
Learning portfolios can turn the learning process into a product (something to manifest in various forms and that can be kept) and treats learning products (achievement) as a process that transforms the learner over time. By maintaining a language learning portfolio, students can archive work in progress or showcase what they are most proud of, demonstrate their proficiency multimodally, and monitor and reflect on the progress they have made. The portfolio is a powerful tool, when used actively and constantly, that relates to all categories and many indicators of learning presence as presented by Shea and Bidjerano (2010), such as forethought and planning (goal setting and planning), monitoring (evaluating quality, noting completion, recognizing learning behaviors), strategy use (recognizing knowledge or skill gap, reviewing), and reflection (see table 7.1). Electronic portfolios, especially online portfolios, can seamlessly present all media in a visually aesthetic platform ready to share at different levels of openness. The electronic format also makes it easier for students to update and maintain their portfolios.

Suggested Tools

- Specific language portfolio platforms such as LinguaFolio, European Language Portfolio, and Global Language Portfolio
- E-portfolio platforms available in learning management systems such as Canvas, CourseNetworking (CN Posts), and itslearning
- Web-based platforms such as Wix, Google Sites, and Weebly

Scaffolding

Teachers can determine the scope of portfolios based on the learning goals of the course or program. They can scaffold by guiding students through categories that are common across portfolios, including the following:

- *Language biography:* brief biography of one's language experiences (e.g., languages spoken and being learned, goals for learning the languages)
- *Language passport:* documentation of language proficiency through copies of diplomas, certificates, and awards, as well as a self-assessment grid based on the current proficiency level. Students can continue to add new self-assessment grids as they make progress.
- *Language experiences:* résumé-like list of major valuable language learning experiences, such as serving as an interpreter for a community event or studying abroad
- *Reflections:* series of professional and personal reflections on the portfolio artifacts and process

Maintaining a working portfolio requires learners to constantly monitor their progress and evaluate their proficiency level. This process can be enhanced by guiding students to use language proficiency self-assessment tools such as the National Council of State Supervisors for Languages (NCSSFL)-ACTFL Can-Do Statements, the self-assessment grid from the Common European Framework of Reference for Languages, and English language proficiency checklists for young learners.

Teachers should provide guidance on how to control different levels for sharing language portfolios. Students can share certain samples with their teachers only and other samples (usually showcase samples) with the general public.

Conclusion

In this chapter, we focus on the rationale for learning presence and suggestions for how teachers can engage students by using learning presence and, most importantly, supporting language learners to enact the presence. The suggestions cover various ways to design instruction and content to support language learners as they take charge of their own learning in the online medium.

> Links for all online resources mentioned in this chapter can be found on the companion site for this book (www.tesol.org/engageonline).

References

Allwright, D. (1998). Contextual factors in classroom language learning: An overview. In K. Malmkoer & J. Williams (Eds.), *Context in language learning and language understanding* (pp. 115–134). Cambridge University Press.

Benson, P. (2007). Autonomy in language teaching and learning. *Language Teaching, 40*(1), 21–40. https://doi.org/10.1017/S0261444806003958

Brooks, C. F., & Young, S. L. (2011). Are choice-making opportunities needed in the classroom? Using self-determination theory to consider student motivation and learner empowerment. *International Journal of Teaching and Learning in Higher Education, 23*(1), 48–59.

Cook-Sather, A. (2006). Sound, presence, and power: "Student voice" in educational research and reform. *Curriculum Inquiry, 36*(4), 359–390. https://doi.org/10.1111/j.1467-873X.2006.00363.x

Holec, H. (1981). *Autonomy and foreign language learning*. Pergamon.

Little, D. (2001). Learner autonomy and the challenge of tandem language learning via the internet. In A. Chambers & G. Davies (Eds.), *Information and communications technology and language learning: A European perspective* (pp. 29–38). Swets & Zeitlinger.

Murray, G. (2014). *Social dimensions of autonomy in language learning*. Palgrave Macmillan.

Pool, J., Reitsma, G., & Van den Berg, D. (2017). Revised community of inquiry framework: Examining learning presence in a blended mode of delivery. *Online Learning Journal, 21*(3): 153–165. http://dx.doi.org/10.24059/olj.v21i3.866

Rasinski, T. (n.d.). *Useful resources: Multidimensional fluency rubric chart*. Tim Rasinski. http://www.timrasinski.com/resources.html

Shea, P., & Bidjerano, T. (2010). Learning presence: Towards a theory of self-efficacy, self-regulation, and the development of a community of inquiry in online and blended learning environments. *Computers in Education, 55*, 1721–1731. https://doi.org/10.1016/j.compedu.2010.07.017

Shea, P., Hayes, S., Uzuner Smith, S., Vickers, J., Bidjerano, T., Gozza-Cohen, M., Jian, S., Pickett, A., Wilde, J., & Tseng, C. (2013). Online learner self-regulation: Learning presence viewed through quantitative content- and social network analysis. *The International Review of Research in Open and Distance Learning, 14*(3), 428–461. https://doi.org/10.19173/irrodl.v14i3.1466

Wang, C., & Burris, M. A. (1997). Photovoice: Concept, methodology, and use for participatory needs assessment. *Health Education & Behavior, 24*(3), 3690387. https://doi.org/10.1177/109019819702400309

Part III

The Next Steps to Sustain Online Teaching Expertise

CHAPTER 8

Exemplary and Inspirational Online Teaching Practices

By Faridah Pawan

In this chapter, we share inspirational practices for online teaching from the work of Martin et al. (2019), Savery (2005), and Pelz (2004). Their influence is evident in the ideas and suggestions throughout this book.

Award-Winning Online Instructional Practices

Martin et al. (2019) interviewed nine award-winning online instructors from across multiple disciplines. These instructors were recognized for their online teaching effectiveness by professional organizations such as the Online Learning Consortium, the Association for Educational Communications and Technology, and the United States Distance Learning Association. Table 8.1 provides examples of award-winning practices for different areas of focus.

VOCAL

Based on many years of online teaching experiences and research, Savery (2005) provided a useful mnemonic—VOCAL (visible, organized, compassionate, analytical, and are leaders by example)—to summarize the key characteristics and practices of effective online teachers. Table 8.2 provides his rationale for developing practices along the lines of these characteristics; we have included accompanying suggestions.

Table 8.1. *Award-Winning Online Teacher Practices*

Areas of focus	Example practices
Online course design	1. Systematic organization (e.g., created learning "road maps" that included learning objectives, modular and weekly course topics, and resources in multiple formats) 2. Backward design (e.g., began with learning outcomes and used them as a basis for creating learning activities and assessments and selecting technology) 3. Course organization (e.g., chunking course content meaningfully and expressing expectations for each of the chunks so students can situate where they are in the learning process) 4. Meeting learner needs (e.g., assessing learners so that appropriate and varied materials can be included) 5. Student interaction (e.g., structuring student interactions and opportunities for avid discussions, collaborative projects, and review; creating community through various media)
Online course assessment	1. Variety of course assessments (e.g., using multiple technologies at different intervals for assessment, including peer assessments, self-assessments, and reflection, as well as a variety of quizzes that provide immediate feedback and are timed or open book) 2. Traditional and authentic assessments (e.g., allowing students to choose and/or create their content digitally to demonstrate learning) 3. Rubrics (e.g., making expectations clear for the class while also helping students track their progress)
Online course evaluation	1. Quality assurance (e.g., seeking the support of colleagues from across disciplines, such as subject matter experts, multimedia designers, etc.) 2. Student and peer feedback (e.g., using analytics from the learning management systems to supplement student evaluations)
Online course facilitation	1. Timely response and feedback (e.g., responding to messages within 24 to 48 hours) 2. Availability and presence (e.g., engaging actively at the beginning of the course and focusing more on formative assessment feedback later) 3. Periodic communication (e.g., sharing announcements at regular and expected intervals)

Source: Adapted from Martin et al. (2019).

"Guide on the Side"

Bill Pelz (2004) won the Sloan Consortium Excellence in Online Teaching Award in 2004, at the beginning of the online boom. His principles of effective online teaching, however, remain relevant and on point to this day. They include the following:

- *Let students do most of the work.* Pelz's transition from "sage on the stage" to "guide on the side" as an online teacher came about with the realization that the "more quality time students spend engaged in the content, the more content they learn" (2004, p. 103).

Table 8.2. *VOCAL in Practice Rationale*

Characteristics	Why does it matter in online practice?
1. Visible	Teacher visibility lets students know that teachers are paying attention and to become acquainted with teachers to establish working relationships; consequently, students are unlikely to be passive. *Suggestion: Use Bitmojis.*
2. Organized	Online environments necessitate self-regulated learning. Thus, learners need to know what is expected of them ahead of time so they or their support systems at home can plan and anticipate how to proceed. *Suggestion: Use the online calendar feature.*
3. Compassionate	Online environments blur physical boundaries and can feel more intimate. Students may be able to share more of themselves. *Suggestion: Develop and enforce netiquette rules.*
4. Analytical	Even though online environments can allow both teachers and students to track progress, students do not have as much external input. Teachers need to provide timely feedback so students can monitor and be assured of their progress. *Suggestion: Embed assessment throughout instruction.*
5. Leader by example	The teacher in the online environment sets the tone for the online classroom community. *Suggestion: Use public and private channels to guide communication.*

Source: Adapted from Savery (2005).

- *Let interactivity be the heart and soul of asynchronous learning.* In this book, interactivity is also central in synchronous learning.

- *Strive for presence.* Pelz referred to the teaching, cognitive, and social presences covered in chapters 4 through 6. We have also incorporated Shea and Bidjerano's (2010) learning presence, which is covered in chapter 7.

Conclusion

These experienced instructors' insights underscore that teachers' pedagogical knowledge and skills are the driving forces in using technology to achieve effective and motivating online teaching. They demonstrate that teachers not only teach but also motivate by inspiring their students.

> Links for all online resources mentioned in this chapter can be found on the companion site for this book (www.tesol.org/engageonline).

References

Martin, F., Ritzhaupt, A., Kumar, S., & Budhrani, K. (2019). Award-winning faculty online teaching practices: Course design, assessment and evaluation, and facilitation. *The Internet and Higher Education, 42*, 34–43. https://doi.org/10.1016/j.iheduc.2019.04.001

Pelz, B. (2004). (My) Three principles of effective online pedagogy. *Journal of Asynchronous Learning Networks, 8*(3), 33–46.

Savery, J. R. (2005). Be vocal: Characteristics of successful online instructors. *Journal of Interactive Online Learning, 4*(2), 141–152.

Shea, P., & Bidjerano, T. (2010). Learning presence: Towards a theory of self-efficacy, self-regulation, and the development of a community of inquiry in online and blended learning environments. *Computers in Education, 55*, 1721–1731. https://doi.org/10.1016/j.compedu.2010.07.017

CHAPTER 9

Ways Administrators Can Use Online Pathways to Reconceptualize and Support Teachers' Professional Development

By Faridah Pawan and Mika Mokko

In this chapter, we turn our attention to teachers' need for support from administrators in transitioning to online learning. We discuss a reconceptualized framework consisting of factors to include in effective online teacher professional development (PD) programs and offer principles and a suggested model for online teacher PD.

As is the case for their students, teachers are motivated by a sense of increased understanding, purpose, and effectiveness that propels them to pursue further professional education. Crandall (1993) identifies the latter as "professionalization," a "time-limited status enhancement through certification or credentialing, contracts, and tenure" (pp. 499–500). She defines professionalism, by contrast, as a lifelong learning process in which teachers are motivated to sustain their learning and enhance the quality of their practice.

To maintain and sustain their expertise, teachers continuously pursue PD, as teacher knowledge is one form of dialectical knowledge. The knowledge develops, evolves, and is mediated by what teachers know about (a) the subject matter, (b) themselves as people and as learners, (c) their students, (d) the learning taking place in their classroom, (e) the micro-school culture within which they work, and (f) the macro community in which they, their students, and their schools are situated (Johnson, 2006). These factors require teachers to continuously "reconceptualize and recontextualize their understandings" (Johnson & Golombek, 2003, p. 735) of thinking and engaging in all aspects of teaching and learning.

In this chapter, we provide practical suggestions for administrators to consider as they look for ways to support online teaching. These suggestions include reconceptualizing PD; establishing principles that guide the development of online PD program development and a model that exemplifies these principles; encouraging the use of personal learning networks (PLNs) that can supplement PD; and consulting with online teachers to guide administrators' next steps in PD.

PD Reconceptualization

Mika Mokko's (2018) survey of professional development needs depicted the views of 27 practicing TESOL teachers who participated extensively in online PLNs. They used a PLN regularly (between three and four hours each week) for a sustained time of more than three years. The teachers also used a minimum of 10 tools (e.g., Twitter or other social media sites, blogs, Ning). Teachers' responses to Mokko's questionnaire led us to develop a reconceptualization of PD programs that expands on two widely recognized PD frameworks—namely, Darling-Hammond and colleagues' (cited in Mokko & Pawan, 2021) framework developed for the U.S.-based Learning Policy Institute and Richardson and Diaz Maggioli's (cited in Mokko & Pawan, 2021) framework specifically for English language teachers worldwide. PD needs to be reconceptualized because the online medium has affected how teachers learn as well as how they are motivated to stay engaged professionally.

In this chapter, we describe this reconceptualization based on the teacher responses that Mokko received and those that we reported previously (Mokko & Pawan, 2021). Our PD model of concentric circles (see fig. 9.1) showcases Darling-Hammond and colleagues' effective PD principles of all teachers in the center. The second circle incorporates Richardson and Diaz Maggioli's principles specific for English language teachers. In the outermost circle, we identify the factors that further expand on the existing two models and thus reconceptualize effective teacher PD when the online medium is taken into consideration. This figure was based on the 2019 Pawan and Mokko model (cited in Mokko & Pawan, 2021).

As in Darling-Hammond and colleagues' and Richardson and Diaz Maggioli's models (fig. 9.1), time is a key PD factor in our model. However, we stress that in online environments, immediacy ("just-in-timeness") provides teachers with ready access to professional support without fear of prolonged separation from sources of expertise and information.

We also subscribe to Garrison's (cited in Mokko & Pawan, 2021) assertion that the online medium demands reflection because of the ability to "arrest" and "freeze" thoughts that were once ephemeral. Thus, by its very nature, the online medium enables teachers to reflect on individual information alone or in the virtual company of others. In that regard, our model reasserts the importance of PD activities that promote reflective engagement, which is advocated as well by Darling-Hammond and colleagues' and Richardson and Diaz Maggioli's frameworks (fig. 9.1).

Accordingly, connectivity, or the "connective-focused" feature in Mokko and Pawan's (2021) framework, is prioritized in our model, whereas in Darling-Hammond and colleagues' model, content-focused sources and opportunities are important for PD (see fig. 9.1). The connective capacity of the online medium provides teachers with not only ideas but also access to colleagues beyond teachers' immediate circles. In our research, we also observed that online connectivity helped minimize teachers' sense of personal isolation for those in remote areas or who teach a language that is not their

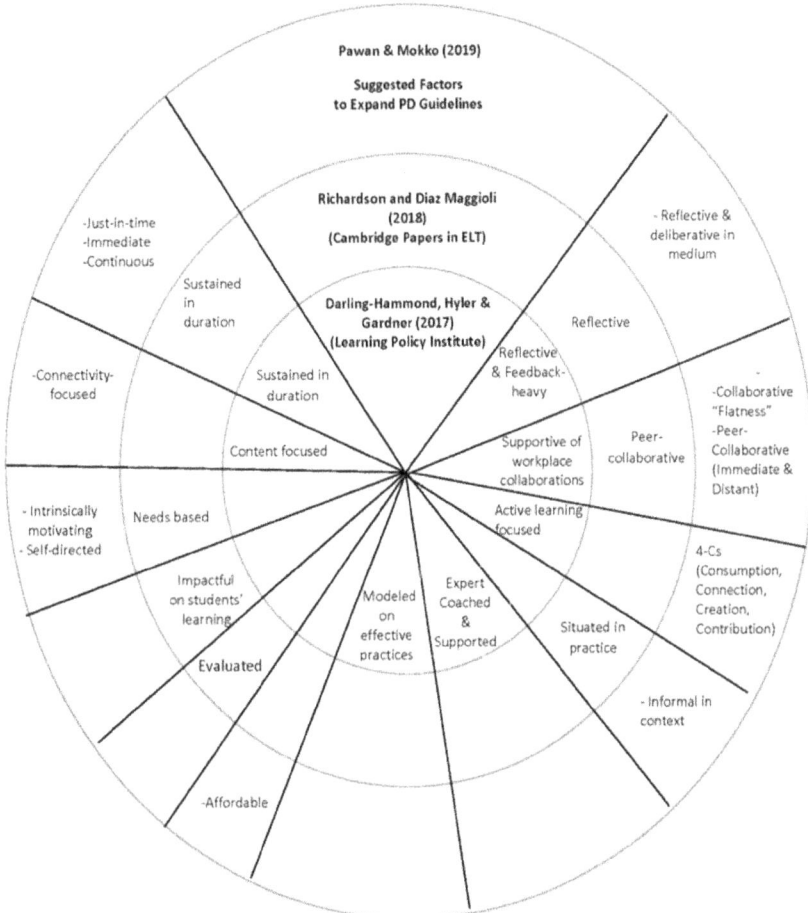

Note: An extended version of the study can be found in Mokko & Pawan (2021).

Figure 9.1. Reconceptualization of TESOL teachers' professional development

native language. Online connectivity also contributed to minimizing teachers' sense of professional marginalization from colleagues who teach "mainstream" subjects and populations.

Connectivity is often most directly related to collaboration, a critical feature of teacher PD in all three models (see fig. 9.1). However, the "flatness" (Friedman, 2005) of the collaboration, where everyone is considered equally informative, stands out when PD is undertaken online. The following quote is illustrative:

> I feel like what's really amazing is that even "big names" join in. . . . For example, when I took an iTDi course, I was reading one of Krashen's articles, and I posted something, and he replied directly. (Caroline, December 2015, quoted in Mokko & Pawan, 2021)

The quote also demonstrates that the online medium can provide invitations and opportunities that may be less available offline.

The online environment lends itself as an inviting place to informally and freely create, share, and, most importantly, "pay it forward" or give back (LaGarde & Whitehead, cited in Mokko & Pawan, 2021). These PD features can increase PD's purpose and meaning. Our findings reflect the four cyclical stages of sustained online engagement: (1) consumption, (2) connection, (3) creation, and (4) contribution stages (Milligan et al., cited in Mokko & Pawan, 2021), with Stages 3 and 4 giving the most satisfaction and incentive to remain engaged.

The absence of an external and outside evaluation of online PD in Mokko and Pawan's (2021) model, in comparison to Richardson and Diaz Maggioli's framework, requires explanation. This absence can be better understood because the online medium enables teachers to pursue online PD opportunities on their terms and allows them to have full control of their learning. Effective teachers are well grounded in their knowledge of their students and able to assess their own professional needs. This ability is the main evaluation criterion mentioned by teachers in the study and one they can use independently when deciding whether to pursue PD online.

Finally, the PD model in Mokko and Pawan (2021) acknowledges the affordability of pursuing online professional development. The prohibitive cost of on-site professional development conferences can be almost roughly equal to the "monthly net salary of a post-doc in the UK," according to Kirchherr and Biswas (cited in Mokko & Pawan, 2021), after the costs of registration, membership, travel, lodging, and meals are considered. From this perspective, online PD offered a more affordable PD alternative to the teachers in the study.

The elements in the reconceptualized PD framework illustrate that the online medium has much to offer teachers seeking PD. From the research, the capabilities of the online medium have provided new ways for teachers to improve their practice.

Principles of Effective PD for Online Teachers and a PD Model as Illustration

As we mentioned earlier in the book, when the 2020 emergency remote teaching mandate (Hodges et al., 2020) forced schools to close, everyone—including administrators and teachers—had anywhere from two days to two weeks to develop and teach online lesson plans. Their efforts were monumental and heroic; their resiliency and creativity continue to inspire. Over time, to sustain this growth and refine current efforts, existing PD programs for online teachers can serve as models for online teaching in the future.

In our opinion, the most effective models for online PD encompass the following principles:

- *Adult learning patterns:* There are two concepts often associated with learning as adults—andragogy and heutagogy. Andragogy posits that adult learning is characterized by autonomous and independent learning (Knowles, 1984). Heutagogy (Kenyon & Hase, 2001) is self-determined learning that comes about with the full expectation that no one knows everything nor has all the answers.

Thus, adults identify for themselves professional development needs to be addressed. In both perspectives, adults are self directed and goal oriented and bring with them substantial experience and knowledge that they apply to new learning experiences (Knowles et al., 1998). Adults engage better when they are involved in the planning and cultivation of their learning; the relevance of what they are learning, why they are learning it, and how it benefits teachers in real-life situations are essential to engagement. Intrinsic motivation for teachers to pursue and engage in professional development programs requires the programs' alignment to andragogy and heutagogy principles.

- *Mediated learning:* Learning is seen as a mediated process in which learners interact with a "more knowledgeable other" (MKO; Vygotsky, 1978) or a "temporary other" (Johnson & Golombek, 2016). An MKO can be anyone working alongside the learner who possesses a higher or better understanding or ability. A temporary other, on the other hand, is a peer who shares similar ability levels or interests, vision, or circumstances with the learner. The mediation enables learners to reach Vygotsky's zone of proximal development, through which they can achieve beyond what they are unable to achieve alone. The process of mediation posits that there are three types of mediators (Kozulin, 2003). The first is the human mediator (e.g., the MKO). The second is the psychological or symbolic mediator (e.g., the system of knowledge and skills). The third is the external mediator, which would include the technical tools that are involved in the process of social interaction (e.g., a computer).

- *Communities of practice (CoP):* Members of a CoP are practitioners at every level of expertise. They develop a shared repertoire of resources—experiences, stories, tools, and ways of addressing recurring problems; in short, they create a shared practice. They engage in sustained interaction over time (Wenger, 2000). Learning in a community of like-minded people builds relationships that affect learning and provides a space to come together. Participation is a bedrock of the community, and individuals are encouraged to engage in and contribute to the community's practices (Wenger, 2000). Time spent in the community provides opportunities for the learners to grow their own culture of practice.

Vaill and Testori (cited in Mokko & Pawan, 2021) describe an online faculty development program at the Center for Distributed Learning (CDL) at Bay Path College, in which the three principles discussed earlier can be seen in convergence in a three-tiered approach:

1. *Cohort training using instructors' existing approaches, courses, and materials:* Teachers engage as cohort groups in working sessions that involve both pedagogical and technical knowledge. Although the sessions' content has predetermined critical topics, the topics are contextualized within the approaches and materials the instructors brought with them to the center. The teachers are part of the force driving the PD support they are being offered, as it is contextualized within their current knowledge and efforts.

2. *Peer mentoring:* Teachers have assigned mentors (experienced and successful online faculty), along with direct access to instructional designers. They observe and take part in the mentors' classes.

3. *Ongoing collaborative support through CoP:* The teachers receive sustained support from the CDL staff members who are directed to check regularly on instructors' classes, provide constructive feedback and assistance, and share ideas on pedagogy and technology. There is also ongoing support from the community they established in steps 1 and 2. (It should be noted here that the CDL staff also support students' technological needs so faculty can focus on online teaching.)

The CDL example can serve as a template for developers creating programs within an existing infrastructure. The program is based on principles that have proven effective in ensuring long-term learning by adults.

Ongoing Needs of Online Teachers

As administrators support online teachers, uncovering teachers' continuing needs is an essential task. Understanding those needs enables administrators to not only target their efforts to develop an infrastructure of support but also encourage the teachers in their work. Administrators' backing and empathy motivate teachers to improve their practices, take risks, and pursue new challenges. The 2019 research report by Martin and colleagues (cited in Mokko & Pawan, 2021) generates useful information that provides insight into online instructors' needs (see table 9.1).

Conclusion

As is evident in the previous chapters and table 9.1, effective PD programs for online teachers need substantial encouragement and support from administrators so that online instruction can capitalize on its unique capabilities. The circumstances of the COVID-19 pandemic in 2020 and the rapid shift to online instruction in many school systems have presented major challenges for teachers and school systems. With the thoughtful development of new PD programs for teachers in online education, however, these challenges can be turned into new learning opportunities for teachers as well as students.

> Links for all online resources mentioned in this chapter can be found on the companion site for this book (www.tesol.org/engageonline).

Table 9.1. *Professional Development Needs of U.S. Online Instructors*

Support themes	Specific support needs coded and identified
Administrative support	More time (e.g., preparation, interaction with students
	Decreased class size
	Credit for teaching online
Teaching support	Course development included in teaching load
	Quality recognized in online teaching courses
Personnel support	Design and development support staff (e.g., instructional designer, technician, multimedia designer, coders, and programmers)
	Faculty peer mentor
	Faculty learning community (e.g., sharing what worked and did not work, insights from experienced instructors)
	Student teaching assistant
Pedagogical support	Teaching strategies (e.g., how to write objectives, how to facilitate online, how to manage time, how to set up group work)
	Instructional resources (e.g., video tutorials, how-to checklists, access to examples)
Technology support	Technical support (access to tech support, just-in-time support)
	Software for video creation
	Hardware (e.g., cameras, headsets)

Source: Adapted from Martin et al. (2019), as cited in Mokko & Pawan (2021).

References

Crandall, J. (1993). Professionalism and professionalization of adult ESL literacy. *TESOL Quarterly, 27*(3), 497–515. https://www.jstor.org/stable/3587479

Friedman, T. L. (2005). *The world is flat: A brief history of the twenty-first century.* Farrar, Straus, and Giroux. http://www.worldcat.org/oclc/57202171

Hodges, C., Moore, S., Lockee, B., Trust, T., & Bond, A. (2020, March 27). The difference between emergency remote teaching and online learning. *EDUCAUSE Review.* https://er.educause.edu/articles/2020/3/the-difference-between-emergency-remote-teaching-and-online-learning

Johnson, K. E. (2006). The sociocultural turn and its challenges for second language teacher education. *TESOL Quarterly, 40*(1), 235–257. https://doi.org/10.2307/40264518

Johnson, K. E., & Golombek, P. R. (2003). "Seeing" teacher learning. *TESOL Quarterly, 37,* 729–738. https://doi.org/10.2307/3588221

Johnson, K. E., & Golombek, P. R. (2016). *Mindful L2 teacher education: A sociocultural perspective on cultivating teachers' professional development.* Routledge Taylor Francis. https://doi.org/10.4324/9781315641447

Kenyon, C., & Hase, S. (2001). *Moving from andragogy to heutagogy in vocational education.* https://eric.ed.gov/?id=ED456279

Knowles, M. S. (1984). *Andragogy in action.* Jossey-Bass. http://www.worldcat.org/oclc/10948662

Knowles, M. S., Holton, E. G., & Swanson, R. A. (1998). *The adult learner: The definitive classic in adult education and human resources development.* Gulf.

Kozulin, A. (2003). Psychological tools and mediated learning. In A. Kozulin, B. Gindis, V. S. Ageyev, & S. M. Miller (Eds.), *Vygotsky's educational theory in cultural context* (pp. 15–38). Cambridge University Press. https://doi.org/10.1017/CBO9780511840975

Martin, F., Wang, C., Budhrani, K., Moore, R. L., & Jokiaho, A. (2019). Professional development support for the online instructor: Perspectives of U.S. and German instructors. *Online Journal of Distance Learning Administration, 22*(3), 1–15. https://digitalcommons.odu.edu/stemps_fac_pubs/99

Mokko, M. (2018). *A qualitative multi-case study of ESL teachers' professional development and their use of personal learning networks* [Unpublished doctoral dissertation/master's thesis]. Indiana University.

Mokko, M., & Pawan, F. (2021). Working toward a reconceptualization of effective TESOL teachers' professional development through "personal learning networks." *Journal of Global Literacies, Technologies, and Emerging Pedagogies, VII*(1), 1335–1349.

Vygotsky, L. S. (1978). *Mind in society: The development of higher psychological processes* (M. Cole, V. John-Steiner, S. Scribner, & E. Souberman, Eds. & Trans.). Harvard University Press.

Wenger, E. (2000). Communities of practice and social learning systems. *Organ, 7*(2), 225–246. https://doi.org/10.1177/135050840072002

CHAPTER 10

Culturally and Linguistically Inclusive Online Instruction

By Faridah Pawan

Teachers are socioprofessionals (Freeman, 2009). Although we begin in our classrooms, our professional communities, our sense of effectiveness, and our sense of mission and motivation are sustained by our ability to connect, reach out, and have an impact beyond the classroom. The pandemic has brought forth our sense of urgency to work with our students to sustain their achievement and progress, even though we have been distanced from them. However, as teachers of language learners, issues related to inclusivity are always foremost in our minds. We teach learners of diverse backgrounds, so we have a responsibility to teach equitably and responsively. To do so, teachers continuously strive to engage our learners in ways that enable them to feel included culturally and linguistically. This sensibility and responsibility follow us as we teach across all media, including in the online environment.

The book concludes with descriptions of two resources to help teachers engage students in an inclusive way:

- A self-paced, free online professional development course on culturally and linguistically inclusive online instruction to support teachers in this endeavor. We developed the course as a free online resource to support our fellow teachers wherever they are, in any way we can. The course was funded by the 2020–2021 Indiana Governor's Emergency Education Relief Fund.

- Recommendations for TESOL's Professional Learning Networks, which can serve as teachers' personal lifelong learning communities.

Culturally and Linguistically Inclusive Online Professional Development Course

The culturally and linguistically inclusive online teaching course was developed for all K–12 teachers whose online classrooms include English learners (ELs) of culturally and linguistically diverse backgrounds. This course supports the teachers by sharing strategies and resources for them to use as they design and implement their own online instruction for these students.

At the most intense time of the pandemic in 2020, Sugarman & Lazarin (2020) reported that less than half of ELs logged into online instruction. Although there are many factors involved with this outcome, two causes are engagement and motivation. This course can help change these outcomes because for ELs to be motivated and engaged in learning online, they must feel included culturally and linguistically. Online teaching must move toward a design that reflects and encompasses the "diversity of learner experiences, including differences in age, gender, cultural background, education, language, socioeconomic status, family and employment commitments, goals, objectives, needs, desires and access to technology" (Gunawardena et al., 2019, p. 9).

The course design team consists of an interdisciplinary group of six individuals: Faridah Pawan, Angela Lankford, Zixi Li, Karen Sue Pollard, Jinzhi Zhou, and Yichuan Yan (table 10.1). They bring expertise in English as a foreign language (EFL) and English as a second language (ESL) teachers' professional development, inclusive online instruction, ESL K–12 teaching, instructional systems technology, and learning sciences. The diversity of the expertise and backgrounds of the individuals strengthens the course design.

Overall Design

- The course is free for all teachers. (The Governor's Emergency Education Relief Fund makes this possible.)
- The course is online and self-paced.
- Completion of this workshop should take approximately 8 to 10 hours.
- All resources are provided in the course.
- Teachers are invited to contribute ideas to the course they are trying.
- Teachers can connect with other teachers through the course if they would like to create a community of practice.

Overall Principles

The course begins with the acknowledgment that as human beings, teachers all carry implicit biases that we need to be aware of and address. This acknowledgment is important because the assumptions we may hold about students can negatively impact our students' growth and success (Staats et al., 2018). Teachers are then directed to reflect on these biases with the help of the Implicit Association Test created by Harvard University's Project Implicit (https://implicit.harvard.edu/implicit/takeatest.html).

Table 10.1. *Course Designers for a Culturally and Linguistically Inclusive Online Teaching Course*

	Faridah Pawan is a professor of EFL/ESL teacher professional development in the Department of Instructional Systems Technology at Indiana University (IU). Since 2004, she has developed multiple online programs, including IU's EFL/ESL teaching and teacher training certificates and the EFL/ESL Online Peace Corps Masters International Program, as well as hybrid programs, such as the Tandem Certification of ESL/Content Area Teachers.
	Angela Lankford is a doctoral student in literacy, language, and culture education, with a minor in adult education, at Indiana University. She regularly provides consultations on inclusive and intercultural online instruction, and her previous experiences include serving as a college writing instructor, teaching in-person and online courses, and working as an adult literacy instructor. She is now a senior learning content writer for a nonprofit online university
	Zixi Li is a doctoral student in instructional systems technology at Indiana University. She earned a bachelor's degree in communication from the University of Washington and a master's degree in information science from the University of Michigan. Her research interest is the blended intelligence between humans and technology in the education field.
	Karen Sue Pollard is an elementary school educator with more than 12 years of experience, including time in Hong Kong, Finland, the New York and New Jersey area, and Indiana. She earned degrees in music education and general education and is currently pursuing a master's degree in literacy, culture, and language education.
	Jinzhi Zhou is a doctoral student in the learning sciences program in the School of Education at Indiana University. She completed her master's degree in new media and new literacies at the University of Michigan. She also has worked as a Chinese language instructor in China, the United Kingdom, and Brazil.
	Yichuan Yan is a doctoral student in the instructional systems technology program at Indiana University. Before attending graduate school, he was a K–16 Chinese language instructor. He currently teaches online courses for the computer educator's license program in the School of Education at Indiana University.

The course then provides an overview of the following pedagogical principles that contextualize its approach and content:

- Culturally responsive teaching (CRT; Gay, 2000; Ladson-Billings, 1995)
- Funds of knowledge (González et al., 2005)
- Second language teaching pedagogy and sheltered instruction (Echevarria et al., 2017)
- Effective online teaching pedagogy (Garrison et al., 2000; Shea & Bidjerano, 2010)

Course Organization, Components, and Examples

There are seven modules to the class:

- Module 1 provides a context for culturally and linguistically inclusive online instruction.
- Modules 2 through 5 provide CRT- and culture-fronted online activities and tools.
- Modules 6 and 7 provide second language and language-fronted online activities and tools.

Figure 10.1 offers a quick overview of one module and its components.

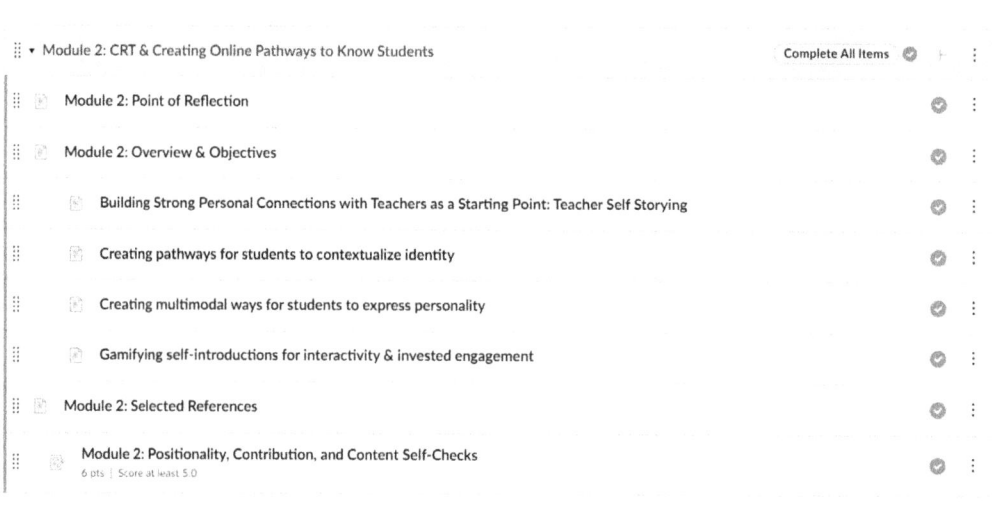

Figure 10.1. Sample module and components from a culturally and linguistically inclusive online teaching course

Each module consists of the following:

- A critical reflection to trigger the need for the activities suggested. In this module, Jane Medina's (1999) poem was used to quickly demonstrate an inequity in teacher expectations. The message here is that teachers must reach out to students to get to know them.

   > Teacher?
   > George, please call me "Mrs. Roberts."
   > Yes, Teacher.
   > George, please don't call me "teacher"!
   > Yes, T- I mean, Mrs. Roberts.
   > You see, George, it's a sign of respect to call me by my last name.
   > Yes . . . Mrs. Roberts.
   > Besides, when you say it, it sounds like "t-shirt."
   > I don't want to be turned into a t-shirt!
   > Mrs. Roberts?
   > Yes, George?
   > Please, call me "Jorge."

- A guide to apply and enact CRT principles in the classroom and align the resulting practices to become an effective online teacher. In the case of the example module (Module 2), teachers must strive to create safe spaces for students to share who they are as individuals. A good starting place for all of these activities is with the teacher sharing information about themselves as an invitation for students to reciprocate. This advice is aligned to the work of Rodgers and Raider-Roth (2006), which calls for online teachers to lead by projecting their self-awareness and a strong connection to students as a means of expressing their interpersonal and intellectual leadership in the online classroom.

- A curated collection of suggested online activities and tools. Under the "teacher self storying" category, several suggested online activities are included. When teachers click the category, they see examples such as Story Mapping, Speaking Your "Grand Design," and "Multi-Dimensioning" the Teacher. In Story Mapping, for example, free tools and real teacher examples are provided:
  - *Tool:* ArcGIS StoryMaps: www.esri.com/en-us/arcgis/products/arcgis-storymaps/overview
  - *Example:* Ms. Cleveland's StoryMap: storymaps.arcgis.com/stories/234d1f5ff59f4c06bbbdf62fd6a2c25f

- Teacher self-checks. At the end of every module, teachers are engaged in three self-checks:
  - An implicit bias check associated with the discussions in the module. In the example module, teachers should explore, either alone or with colleagues, the provided resource on "affinity bias," a bias of preferring individuals who are like us.

- A contributions check reminding teachers to upload ideas and suggestions to the course in order to support and continue to enrich the learning of their fellow teachers.
- A content check by taking a quiz on the topic, which they can take as often as they like.

Note: The free online professional development course is available to everyone. The information should be used and disseminated to anyone who might find it useful (expand.iu.edu/browse/office-of-school-partnerships/courses/culturally-and-linguistically-inclusive-online-teaching). If you are not associated with Indiana University, to enter the course, create a guest account at login.iu.edu/guest/new.

TESOL Professional Learning Networks as Personal Lifelong Learning Communities

Pew Research Center (cited in Mokko & Pawan, 2021) reports that in 2019, 90 percent of online American adults used social media: YouTube (73 percent), Facebook (69 percent), Instagram (37 percent), Pinterest (28 percent), LinkedIn (27 percent), Snapchat (24 percent), Twitter (22 percent), WhatsApp (20 percent), and Reddit (11 percent). It is quite evident that adults use social media extensively, so administrators should support the incorporation of these media into teachers' professional development. Dulworth (2008) stated that learning from a social media "network can be more powerful than other types of learning because you are often learning from other people who have 'been there and done that'" (p. 11). He further explained:

> I think there is a shift happening in the world today where people are starting to recognize that in fact, network interactions are one of the keys to learning not only for professionals but for people in general. Because when you have a peer network you hear the story of someone else who is in a similar situation to you so there is almost an immediate validity of what you are hearing because you recognize that this person faces the same problems. There is something about hearing the words of someone who is a peer that makes the relevance of the knowledge that you get very immediate. (Dulworth, 2008, p. 11)

Online communities can provide different approaches to lifelong learning and professional development. Participation in online communities allows users to experience the power of communication in a network or group of like-minded individuals.

Lifelong Learning Through Personal Learning Networks

A personal learning network (PLN) consists of people, tools, or nodes from which a learner obtains knowledge or with which a learner connects. Nussbaum-Beach (cited in Mokko, 2018) defines a PLN as "a reciprocal learning system in which educators participate by sharing with and then learning from others. PLNs are *personal* in the sense that each of us selects our own set of connections as we pursue self-directed, independent, learning experiences, most often online" (p. 1). There are three main PLN types identified by Warlick (cited in Mokko, 2018):

1. Personally maintained synchronous connections
2. Personally and socially maintained semisynchronous connections
3. Dynamically maintained asynchronous connections

Mokko (2018) describes personally maintained synchronous connections as those that include individuals asking and answering questions while at the same time solving problems through tools such as chats, texts, Skype, Zoom, and Twitter to enhance professional development. The semisynchronous PLN type differs from the first in that the connections and collaborations do not take place in real time, but rather during a time when it is most convenient to the users by, for example, commenting on a blog post or commenting on discussion boards. The third asynchronous PLN type, unlike the first two, connects users with content sources or tools that another PLN user has deemed essential or valid to be used and shared. These tools can be applications such as social bookmarking sites or a Really Simple Syndication (RSS), where information is delivered to the reader.

TESOL's Professional Learning Networks

The three PLN types are equally useful for different purposes and depending on teachers' familiarity and comfort. TESOL International Association (2021) has online learning communities that members can select to include as part of their PLNs as well. The communities can be found under the heading of TESOL's Professional Learning Networks (see www.tesol.org/connect/communities-of-practice). They include the following:

- Arts and Creativity
- Assessment Issues
- Black English Language Professionals & Friends
- Career Path Development
- Environmental Responsibility
- Faith in English Language Teaching
- Global Education
- Intensive English Programs
- Palestinian Educators & Friends
- Lesbian, Gay, Bisexual, & Trans
- TESOL Diversity Collaborative
- Video
- Womentorship in ELT

Conclusion

As we approach what we hope is a postpandemic phase, online schools and instruction are "here to stay" (Singer, 2021), as the pandemic has led to paradigm shifts in teaching and learning. For example, Singer (2021) reports that in a study by the RAND Corporation, 20 percent of school administrators said that online schools are now part of their systems and will continue to be so postpandemic. The flexibility that the medium provides is also diminishing the line between classroom-based instruction and virtual learning, formal and informal learning, and learning at home and at school. Accordingly, in the postpandemic era, virtual learning is almost certain to become an important resource for all teachers and parents of ELs to sustain as well as augment instruction within and beyond the classroom walls and beyond the "traditional" school year. Given the affordances of the online medium, teachers now have additional support to enact our responsibility to work together to ensure multiplicity and inclusivity in the voices we include, the needs we address, and the achievements and abilities we recognize and celebrate in our classrooms.

Links for all online resources mentioned in this chapter can be found on the companion site for this book (www.tesol.org/engageonline).

References

Dulworth, M. (2008). *The connect effect: Building strong, personal, professional and virtual networks.* Berrett-Koehler.

Echevarria, J., Vogt, M. E., & Short, D. J. (2017). *Making content comprehensible for English learners: The SIOP Model* (5th ed.). Pearson. https://www.pearson.com/us/higher-education/program/Echevarria-Making-Content-Comprehensible-for-English-Learners-The-SIOP-Model-with-Enhanced-Pearson-e-Text-Access-Card-Package-5th-Edition/PGM2490531.html

Freeman, D. (2009). The scope of second language teacher education. In A. Burns & J. C. Richards (Eds.), *The Cambridge guide to second language teacher education* (pp. 11–19). Cambridge University Press. http://www.worldcat.org/oclc/664310952

Garrison, D. R., Anderson, T., & Archer, W. (2000). Critical inquiry in a text-based environment: Computer conferencing in higher education. *The Internet and Higher Education, 2*(2–3), 87–105.

Gay, G. (2000). *Culturally responsive teaching: Theory, research, & practice.* Teachers College Press. https://www.tcpress.com/culturally-responsive-teaching-9780807758762

González, N., Moll, L., & Amanti, C. (Eds). (2005). *Funds of knowledge: Theorizing practices in households, communities and classrooms.* Erlbaum. https://doi.org/10.4324/9781410613462

Gunawardena, C. N., Frechette, C., & Layne, L. (2019). *Culturally inclusive instructional design: A framework and guide for building online wisdom communities.* Routledge. https://doi.org/10.4324/9781315439204

Ladson-Billings, G. (1995). Toward a theory of culturally relevant pedagogy. *American Educational Research Journal, 32*(3), 465–491. https://doi.org/10.3102/00028312032003465

Medina, J. (1999). *My name is Jorge*. Astra Publishing House.

Mokko, M. (2018). *A qualitative multi-case study of ESL teachers' professional development and their use of personal learning networks* [Unpublished doctoral dissertation/master's thesis]. Indiana University.

Mokko, M., & Pawan, F. (2021). Working toward a reconceptualization of effective TESOL teachers' professional development through "personal learning networks." *Journal of Global Literacies, Technologies, and Emerging Pedagogies, VII*(1), 1335–1349.

Rodgers, C. R., & Raider-Roth, M. B. (2006). Presence in teaching. *Teachers and Teaching: Theory and Practice, 12*(30), 265–287. https://doi.org/10.1080/13450600500467548

Shea, P., & Bidjerano, T. (2010). Learning presence: Towards a theory of self-efficacy, self-regulation, and the development of a community of inquiry in online and blended learning environments. *Computers in Education, 55*, 1721–1731. https://doi.org/10.1016/j.compedu.2010.07.017

Singer, N. (2021, April 11). Online schools are here to stay, even after the pandemic. *The New York Times.* https://www.nytimes.com/2021/04/11/technology/remote-learning-online-school.html

Staats, B. R., KC, D., & Gino, F. (2018). Maintaining beliefs in the face of negative news: The moderating role of experience. *Management Science, 64*(2), 804–824. https://doi.org/10.1287/mnsc.2016.2640

Sugarman, J., & Lazarin, M. (2020). *Educating English learners during the COVID-19 pandemic: Policy ideas for states and school districts*. Migration Policy Institute. https://www.migrationpolicy.org/sites/default/files/publications/mpi-englishlearners-covid-19-final.pdf

TESOL International Association. (2021). *TESOL communities of practice.* https://www.tesol.org/connect/communities-of-practice

About the Authors

Faridah Pawan is a professor of English as a second language (ESL)/English as a foreign language (EFL) teacher professional development in the School of Education at Indiana University-Bloomington (IU SoE). She designs and researches programs to support midcareer professionals to enhance their expertise. In the United States, she developed multiple P–12 teacher ESL professional development projects in 25 Indiana school districts. For a decade, Pawan directed the IU SoE online ESL/EFL Professional Development via Distance Education certificate program. From 2012–2018, Pawan directed the IU online EFL/ESL Peace Corps Masters International Program for teachers. She has also developed similar programs to support teachers in Costa Rica, China, Turkey, the Republic of North Macedonia, India, and several other locations. Pawan has multiple publications, including the coauthored 2017 book *The Pedagogy and Practice of Online Language Teacher Education*, also published by TESOL Press.

Sharon Daley is an associate clinical professor in the Indiana University School of Education. Her primary focus is teaching preservice teachers in literacy methods and field experience courses. She also teaches graduate courses focusing on literacy instruction, assessment, and literacy coaching. Her research interests focus on identity development of preservice teachers, as well as their development as reflective practitioners. She also works on projects to provide courses that develop academic readiness skills in undergraduate students in underserved international populations. Her 20 years in K–6 schools inform her teaching and research.

Xiaojing Kou has served as director for the Center for Language Technology at Indiana University since 2012. With her leadership, the center provides technology and instructional support to language teaching instructors through audio and video services, specialized language instructional space, web hosting of language materials, professional development opportunities, and promotion of world languages programs. She also provides consultation on technology integration in language instructional design and development. She is a member of the Advisory Committee for the Less Commonly Taught and Indigenous Languages Partnership, a cross-university initiative among the Big Ten Academic Alliance. She served as a coach at Hackathon 2020, hosted by the Language Flagship Technology Innovation Center.

Curtis J. Bonk is a professor in the School of Education at Indiana University (IU), teaching psychology and technology courses. Bonk is a former software entrepreneur, CPA, corporate controller, and educational psychologist who presently is an educational technologist, award-winning writer, highly published researcher, statewide and national awardee in innovative teaching with technology, and internationally acclaimed presenter. In 2020, he was awarded the IU President's Award for Excellence in Teaching and Learning Technology, and in 2021, he received the David H. Jonassen Excellence in Research Award. Bonk has written more than 380 publications and given nearly 1,800 talks around the world.

www.ingramcontent.com/pod-product-compliance
Ingram Content Group UK Ltd.
Pitfield, Milton Keynes, MK11 3LW, UK
UKHW050411240426
12048UKWH00020B/1464